GUIDANCE MONOGRAPH SERIES

Shelley C. Stone

Bruce Shertzer

Editors

GUIDANCE MONOGRAPH SERIES

The general purpose of Houghton Mifflin's Guidance Monograph Series is to provide high quality coverage of topics which are of abiding importance in contemporary counseling and guidance practice. In a rapidly expanding field of endeavor, change and innovation are inevitably present. A trend accompanying such growth is greater and greater specialization. Specialization results in an increased demand for materials which reflect current modifications in guidance practice while simultaneously treating the field in greater depth and detail than commonly found in textbooks and brief journal articles.

The list of eminent contributors to this series assures the reader expert treatment of the areas covered. The monographs are designed for consumers with varying familiarity to the counseling and guidance field. The editors believe that the series will be useful to experienced practitioners as well as beginning students. While these groups may use the monographs with somewhat different goals in mind, both will benefit from the treatment given to content areas.

The content areas treated have been selected because of specific criteria. Among them are timeliness, practicality, and persistency of the issues involved. Above all, the editors have attempted to select topics which are of major substantive concern to counseling and guidance personnel.

Shelley C. Stone

Bruce Shertzer

THE COUNSELOR
AND YOUTH
EMPLOYMENT.

WILLIAM C. BINGHAM
RUTGERS UNIVERSITY

HOUGHTON MIFFLIN COMPANY · BOSTON
ATLANTA · DALLAS · GENEVA, ILL. · HOPEWELL, N.J. · PALO ALTO

Library of Congress Catalog Card
Number: 72–1843

DEDICATION

TO JERRY . . .
WHO NEVER KNEW HOW MUCH OF AN
INSPIRATION HE HAS BEEN.

CONTENTS

....

EDITORS' INTRODUCTION

Recent interest in career development as a legitimate and essential function in American education has led to a resurgence of concern about vocational guidance in the schools. This monograph discusses several relevant elements bearing upon the vocational development of youth as they mature.

Dr. Bingham presents a historical perspective of the fate of career-oriented efforts from the beginning of the guidance movement to the present, an overview of vocational theory and vocational development, a discussion of the importance and place of vocational self perceptions of youth and the facilitation of career development within the school. The improvement of school programs to maximize the preparation of youth for the world of work concludes his presentation.

School counselors and other educational personnel interested or involved in the vocational development responsibilities of schools to the youth they serve will find a thorough discussion of the broad sweep of their task in Dr. Bingham's material. The difficulties, challenges and opportunities are covered in a scholarly, readable manner.

SHELLEY C. STONE

BRUCE SHERTZER

AUTHOR'S INTRODUCTION

For nearly 60 years, vocational guidance has been a force in American education. As knowledge of human behavior has expanded, the demands on the time and competencies of practitioners have increased apace. As professional counselors have become more sophisticated, they have been called upon to attend to a wider range of behavior than ever before. The contribution that school counselors make to American youth is expected to grow in both quantity and quality.

Some factors operate to assist counselors in meeting expanded performance criteria. Electronic and photographic equipment are well on the way to making some information and data management problems mechanical operations. The work that was viewed 20 years ago by some counselors as their stock in trade is being taken over by machines. Advancement of these trends will provide counselors with freedom from some routine tasks and access to better data about students than was ever available before. Prospects for the delivery of excellent service are greater than at any time in the past.

At the same time, other forces are afoot that may limit resources, personnel and material alike. Accountability has become a catchword. Budgets are being reduced, or at least not expanded. In some cases, staff members are being reassigned to classroom duties.

The work of school counselors is complex indeed. What better time for them to examine carefully what they do and how they go about it? What better time for them to consider what it is they really want to do? Perhaps this monograph will help in those efforts.

The first section of this monograph presents a brief historical perceptive on vocational guidance in the United States and the roles and functions of counselors in schools. The temptation to title Chapter 1 "Who took the 'vocational' out of guidance?" was resisted, but the content is related to that general theme.

To the extent that counselors get involved with youth employment and preparation for it, a central purpose of their activity ought to be the facilitation of vocational maturity and eventual vocational adjustment. Chapter 2 is concerned primarily with some of the components of vocational maturity, and Chapter 3 presents an examination of vocational self-perceptions.

Although the early literature in vocational psychology tended to treat occupational choice as an isolated event in the lives of workers, prevailing theory today regards occupational choice as a process extending over several years. Taken as a whole, that literature represents an effort to explicate a very complex set of phenomena including demographic variables, human potentialities, the circumstances and conditions of work, worker behaviors and satisfaction, and other personal and environmental factors. Although differential psychology and clinical psychology have been major influences, theorists, researchers, and practitioners concerned with vocational behavior have drawn heavily from other academic disciplines: human development, social psychology, learning theory, sociology, economics, political science, etc. A thorough understanding of vocational behavior, of course, requires careful attention to all of the components and processes of vocational development. Space does not permit full elaboration of all of those considerations here even though their relationship to the employment of youth is obviously important.

The educational system is accused of failing large segments of the student body, and cries are heard at every turn for change and reform. The National Advisory Council on Vocational Education (NACVE, 1972) has recently issued such a call for change in counseling and guidance. That body is concerned with the preparation of young people for employment, as the present monograph is, but their recommendations are too sweeping for all of them to be considered here. Some of them, though, are of interest in this context. They receive attention at suitable points in Chapters 4 and 5. It is in the spirit of making positive suggestions for the improved performance of counselors in relation to the employment of youth that the final two chapters are presented.

With historical trends, role expectations of counselors, and theoretical issues discussed in previous chapters in mind, Chapter 4 reviews some school practices that appear to have made positive contributions to aspects of the preparation of youth for employment. Suggestions are also offered for modification, extension, or abandonment of other practices.

Chapter 5 is devoted to some issues related to the evaluation of guidance services. Of particular concern is the improvement of conceptualization of the service as well as practice.

WILLIAM C. BINGHAM

ACKNOWLEDGEMENTS

To countless students, colleagues, and friends my deep appreciation for stimulating and helping to modify the ideas represented herein. While others helped to form and reform the ideas, responsibility for how they are expressed is mine.

To Margaret Hammond my warm thanks for her tireless efforts in typing the manuscript and for her endless tolerance of my errors.

To my wife, Grace, for being available with support and encouragement when it is needed most, and to Brigitte and Brendan for just being, my love.

1

The Conduct of Vocational Guidance

Even though the last decade has witnessed a renewed interest in vocational guidance, there has been relatively little change in actual guidance practice, especially in public schools. In this chapter, some of the factors which appear to permit or influence operators of guidance programs to neglect or de-emphasize vocational concerns will be examined. They are: the prevailing crisis orientation in guidance; professional influences on counselor behavior; and the fundamental humanness of counselors.

A Historical Perspective

Almost all of the guidance that young people receive before they reach the age of employability occurs in schools. For several decades, leaders in counseling and counselor education have admonished that guidance should have a developmental focus, but school guidance continues to be primarily crisis oriented. Because of that crisis orientation, attention to vocational development is often minimal. This results from the fact that a small proportion of the crises that young people

1

encounter in schools are vocational. When a crisis experience does happen to have vocational meaning, that meaning may very well be overlooked because other more visible components, such as personal or social adjustment or educational achievement, seem to require more immediate attention. Even if a counselor or a teacher is aware of vocational relevance in a crisis, the nature of the crisis, in all likelihood, will restrict opportunities to bring the vocational relevance of the situation into the student's awareness. So long as the central focus of guidance activities is crisis, vocational considerations are apt to be overlooked, or at least reduced to a second-order priority.

But it has not always been that way. Guidance in the United States began with a very decisive vocational orientation. The intention of the first publication in this area (Parsons, 1909) was eminently clear in the title: *Choosing a Vocation.* Parsons translated that intention into action by founding the Vocation Bureau in Boston in 1908. While other cities probably began work in vocational guidance just as early, Boston made greater progress during the early years (Brewer, 1942). Many of the initial efforts to offer vocational guidance were not located in the schools; they were in community agencies similar to the Vocation Bureau. In spite of that separation, the activities of Parsons and others like him paved the way for guidance in the schools. Schools had many of the facilities and resources needed to deliver vocational guidance to the young people who needed it, and there was concern that "the amount and character of the false guidance which goes on is proof enough that the schools and other educational agencies should take up the work." (Brewer, 1918, p. 4). The practice of vocational guidance caught on rapidly and within a decade after the establishment of the Vocation Bureau, schools had taken over much of the service, courses in counselor preparation were available for credit at several universities, and the first national professional association had been organized (Brewer, 1942).

The move toward incorporation of vocational guidance services into school programs was not accompanied by a design to reduce the vocational focus. As a matter of fact, early efforts in that direction often included activities like the conduct of "life-career classes" (Brewer, 1918, p. 142) and emphasized that the primary concern be choice of a vocation (Myers, 1933). The official position of the National Vocational Guidance Association, as adopted in 1924, clearly subsumed educational guidance in its definition of vocational guidance. It also recognized the need to facilitate transition from school to employment for dropouts as well as graduates and advocated that each teacher relate subject matter to occupational life (Brewer, 1926).

In spite of efforts to maintain a primarily vocational emphasis for guidance, it was probably inevitable, as guidance became well established in schools and as trained experts became widely available, that concerns of greater immediacy would command increasing amounts of attention. Formulations appearing during the 1930s foreshadowed events to come. Koos and Kefauver (1932) cited three general functions of guidance: (1) informing students concerning educational and vocational opportunities, (2) securing information about students, and (3) guiding individual students. Although the vocational focus had not disappeared in their formulation, it is clear that the functions they named are somewhat broader than "choosing a vocation." Brewer (1932) saw opportunities to incorporate guidance into a revitalized curriculum, but another leader of the time made an appeal to regard guidance as meaning only vocational guidance because it appeared about to swallow up all of education (Kitson, 1934). Miller (1964) saw the period as one in which preparation for a vocation became just one of the responsibilities of good citizenship about which schools were concerned and prepared to offer service.

The Changing Nature of Guidance

Whatever the reasons, between the two world wars, the nature of guidance in schools did change. Areas of student behavior other than vocational planning consumed larger and larger shares of counselor time. It was not that concern with vocational behavior had diminished. Rather, it was that the intricate relationship of vocational behavior to other areas of behavior was more fully understood than had been the case before. As became broadly manifest in popular textbooks during the decade or so immediately following World War II (e.g., Matthewson, 1949; Tyler, 1961) it was becoming generally recognized that young people cannot always reach educational or vocational objectives unless they have assistance in coping with personal adjustment problems. The growth of clinical psychology during World War II, and its subsequent impact on schools, continued the tendency for vocational guidance to become smothered in a myriad of other behavioral concerns. By 1960, the trends in guidance (Gowan, 1960) indicated movement beyond vocational concepts to all aspects of childhood and movement toward global analysis of people and their problems. As general levels of sophistication in educators increased, more and more of the specialist's time became devoted to student behavior occurring in the present.

A Crisis Orientation

As guidance services developed an increasing emphasis on matters such as effective interpersonal relations, self-understanding, developmental tasks, self-direction, and individual dignity, professional attention to those concerns became consuming. The temptation was certainly strong to neglect or postpone discussion of behavior several years in the future (such as development of job-seeking skills) in favor of attending to some self-understanding crisis ("my mother doesn't love me") occurring in the here and now. How much more dramatic it is to work with a ninth grader fighting to maintain his dignity in a conflict between peer-imposed expectations and family teachings than it is to guide his struggle to internalize data that may eliminate a preferred but unsuitable occupation from serious consideration. How much more satisfying it appears to help a twelfth-grade girl to "understand" that other girls avoid her because she is unpleasant to them than to help her "understand" that she may not be hired if she speaks offensively in a job interview. How much more impelling it is to analyze sex-role behavior from the shyest "first dater" to the most flagrant of promiscuity than it is to witness the unfolding resolution of a sex-role stereotype in an occupational preference. How much more important it seems to deal with what is happening now than what may happen in the future — even if the future is next week, or tomorrow.

The attraction to deal with the immediate may be even more appealing for the student than for the counselor. For the student is involved in his current problems, and he may see their resolution as a matter of personal survival. The need to deal with that concern is immediate, and it must be addressed. So the issue is not really whether it is appropriate to attend to present rather than future events. One often does not have the luxury of that choice anyway. The issue is simply whether counselors want to foster the outcomes that ensue when the standard practice is to address only immediate concerns. Two such outcomes seem likely. First, when it appears to students (and others in the counselor's environment) that only immediate problems get attention in a guidance office, then the expectation develops that the service is intended to address only immediate problems; the operators of the service are seen as "crisis fixers." Second, students' (and others') opportunities to observe planful behavior related to long-range problems is minimized. In either event, the guidance office will not be seen as a place to learn planful behavior. For those who have other opportunities to learn planfulness, this may not be a serious restriction. For those who have no such opportunity to learn planfulness outside of school, it may constitute an irretrievable loss.

The extent of crisis orientation in school guidance may be more pervasive than most counselors realize despite the fact that advocacy of developmental approaches to guidance is common. Counselors "know" that their programs ought to be more developmental, and most of them really want them to be. Data about crisis orientation are not common in the literature. One relevant study is very impressive, however. Davis

(1960) studied how counselors in one state spend their time. He found that 82 percent of the time spent in consultation with parents was associated with emergency and special cases; the other 18 percent were "regularly scheduled" conferences. These data may not be representative, but certainly they are not totally atypical either. Doubtless these same counselors also spend some emergency time with students, teachers, principals, etc. It seems reasonable to conclude that a substantial proportion of the parents in this case see the counselors as "crisis fixers." An unknown number of the other people with whom they interact probably see them the same way.

The extent to which crisis orientation has an impact on the service offered is not well understood. Probably it is more influential on the outcomes of guidance programs than is generally realized. Typically, counselors are reasonably busy people who schedule their time rather fully. When a crisis is addressed, in all likelihood, something else is neglected. If two or three crises happen at the same time, the counselor can easily fall behind in "routine" duties—entering case notes, writing reports, conducting "get acquainted" interviews, writing recommendations, or whatever. As soon as a crisis passes, it is necessary to get back to the rest of the job. Perhaps most of the paper work gets done, but less pressing interviews with clients are postponed. If a number of crises occur in rapid succession, it is possible to get hopelessly behind. Reports are overdue, budget requests are not complete, college and employment recommendations should have been in the mail yesterday. A number of such deadlines can accumulate and upset an otherwise manageable schedule. In extreme cases, the ordinary "paper work" itself becomes a crisis. The counselor becomes a "crisis hopper" skipping peripatetically from one crisis to another and the guidance office takes on appearances of frantic ineffectiveness. Only crises of the most urgent character get attention; everything else is postponed until it too becomes urgent.

If the foregoing description seems grossly exaggerated, one need only visit some guidance offices at certain predictable times (the first and last two or three weeks of the school year, for example) to discover that it is only a mild exaggeration. But the exaggeration is justified to emphasize the point. When crisis orientation prevails, some functions are postponed or perhaps even entirely neglected. Those functions which deal with long-range outcomes are the ones most likely to be neglected. Most vocationally relevant outcomes of guidance are either very much in the future or they are intricately related to educational or personal-social concerns. For those that are long-range, it is almost certain that they will be lost in the shuffle. Those which are mixed up with the visible educational and personal-social concerns will be lost because of the higher urgency attached to the more visible ones. Practically none of the crises which occur in schools are of direct vocational relevance. Thus, in a constant crisis-oriented operation, it is extremely difficult for *vocational* guidance to receive sufficient attention. The survival of *vocational* guidance depends on the planful operation of guidance programs. Counselors are hard pressed to be planful about the programs and services they offer when they try to perform beyond the capacity of the resources at their disposal.

Professional Influences on Counselor Behavior

Historical changes in guidance offerings and crisis-oriented responses of counselors have not been the only influences affecting the proportion of counselor effort directed to vocational concerns. A variety of professional factors have operated as well. An exhaustive analysis of those influences is not possible here, but it is important to examine some of them. This section will consider three important factors: counselor education, professional publications, and convention program content.

Counselor Education

Shortly after the formation of the Vocation Bureau in 1908, courses for the preparation of counselors were being offered on a wide basis (Brewer, 1942). By about 1910, the schools had taken over many vocational guidance functions (Kitson, 1934) and, consequently, influenced the preparation of people who became counselors. The schools also influenced the selection of counselors. Because vocational guidance grew rapidly, course offerings at the college and university level also increased rapidly. Probably quantity grew faster than quality. There was widespread concern about the quality of services being offered (Brewer, 1942) because counselors were not adequately prepared for their work, and they were trying to do guidance in addition to their regular full-time jobs.

Presumably, in the early days of vocational guidance confusion and uncertainty about the preparation of counselors was a function of the "newness" of the occupation. One would like to expect, however, that as the status of the occupation became established, standards of preparation would have achieved some general acceptance. Wrenn (1947) concluded that it was difficult to delineate performance standards because of the indefiniteness of guidance functions, and he found (1957) that authorities were not in agreement as to the roles to be assumed by counselors in schools. In an examination of roles at the college level, Burnett (1954), found need for: (1) clarification of personnel workers' roles, (2) more careful job definition, (3) determination of job competencies, and (4) translation of those competencies into effective training experiences. His conclusions reflected the opinions of many experts of the day. At about the same time, Stoughton (1957) was calling for refinement of training requirements, but found educational institutions lacking in selection procedures. He recommended that selection techniques be devised to increase the probability that only candidates who could succeed be selected for training programs. He also found that though there was agreement on general areas of preparation, there was much diversity in preparation. Hill and Nitzschke (1961) also found a wide variety in course offerings. The professional literature continues to cite lack of agreement about training. Engle and Betz (1971) proposed a two-year program in which they called for the precise definition of the uniqueness or special expertise that the counselor brings to the task.

With somewhat more certainty, but with considerably broader focus, other opinions have been expressed by recognized authorities. Kitson (1934) observed that general guidance is really an attempt to individualize instruction. Arbuckle (1970) expressed the opinion that counselors are in the best position to revolutionize education. Both of these statements indicate directions for guidance that are not necessarily widely accepted.

Clearly, there is anything but unanimity among counselor educators regarding professional preparation. Definitions are unclear, and efforts at refinement of them do not always run in compatible directions. Russell (1960) advocated that one way to improve counselor preparation would be to abandon discussion of some controversies and give students the tools they need and let them resolve the issues for themselves. Lewis and Lewis (1970), on the other hand, made a plea for complete training of counselors rather than depending on them to complete their own readiness at some time after the termination of training. What is expected as the outcome of counselor preparation is not much better defined today than it was many years ago.

Beyond the lack of agreement about general preparation of counselors, it is essentially impossible to determine the emphasis placed on vocational matters in counselor education programs. Often, the only visible evidence is course titles, commonly "Occupational Information" or "Educational and Occupational Information." It can be argued, of course, that attitudes about and uses of information are more important than exposure to it. The exposure is difficult enough to analyze, and it is available information even though its meaning is not always crystal clear.

Information about occupations was one of three elements in Parson's

(1909) formulation of the process of "choosing a vocation," and a related course has usually been included in counselor preparation. MacMinn and Ross (1959) found that 82 percent of the master's programs and 89 percent of the doctoral programs they surveyed included such a course. In 1953 (Jones and Miller, 1954), 29 states required preparation in occupational information for certification as a counselor. More recently, Joseph and Drury (1971) found that most counselors had taken at least one information course. Opinions differ about the adequacy of preparation in this area. In spite of apparently limited attention to vocations, one investigator (Kaplan, 1970) implied that vocational development theory gets more attention than pre-college counseling. His survey of 1174 counselors in four states led to the conclusion that the "popular notion of the school counselor devoting a disproportionate amount of time to pre-college counseling is not supported by the data" (p. 8). In a study of approved training programs for counseling psychologists, Myers (1964) found that 12 of 22 programs offered no more than one course in occupational information. There was wide divergence in the amount of influence of vocational guidance on the curriculum in the programs he studied. He quoted another report (Paterson and Lofquist, 1960) regarding 20 programs of which six emphasized the world of work, nine had little emphasis and five had none.

Official preparation recommendations of both the American School Counselor Association (ASCA, 1964) and Division 17 of the American Psychological Association (Thompson and Super, 1964) appear to lack a clear emphasis on vocations. Of course, both associations prefer preparation which focuses on human development broadly conceived and problem-solving behavior. Thus, vocational behavior is seen as a single aspect of a very complex group of phenomena. But, in general, the preparation of counselors as recommended by these professional associations is more comprehensive than formerly. These associations, of course, are influenced by the same forces that have broadened the scope of guidance services generally. The associated broad scope of training permits vocational concerns to become obscured if not deemphasized.

Professional Publications

The content of a professional journal is either a major influence on the behavior of the occupational group served or an important reflection of its preferences. In either case, some inferences about professional interests can be drawn from the content of professional journals. With that purpose in mind, a perfunctory review was made of two journals: *The School Counselor*, as a primary journal of counselors, and *Counselor Education and Supervision*, as a primary journal for counselor educators.

Counselor Education and Supervision is described in its masthead as a journal "concerned with research, theory development, or program applications pertinent to counselor education and supervision." As such, it publishes articles in its quarterly issues, submitted largely by counselor educators and supervisors (81.5 percent of contributors to Volume 10 were university based), on a wide range of matters relevant to counselor education and supervision. Seven issues of this journal, ranging from the fall of 1970 to the spring of 1972, were examined. Those issues included 69 articles, only 2 of which were obviously addressed to preparation of counselors for some aspect of vocational guidance. Doubtless the content of some other articles would bear on preparation for vocational guidance, but a casual reader (such as a beginning graduate student in counseling or a school administrator) skimming through tables of contents, might be left with the impression that vocational concerns receive relatively little attention.

The School Counselor is described in its masthead as a journal "directed primarily to the interests of practitioners and educators in the field of guidance and counseling, especially those employed in school settings." The eight issues reviewed for present purposes (January, 1971 to May, 1972) contained 72 articles, 22 "Readers Reflections," and 25 items in "Practitioners Potpourri." In these categories, there were, respectively, four, zero, and two entries which had an obviously vocational focus. Again, there is no question but that some other items and articles would have some bearing on practices in vocational guidance. But it is clear that a casual peruser would hardly get the impression that vocational guidance is a high priority of the people served by the journal.

Other journals, of course, are important to the two populations chosen for examination here. One that many of them probably are familiar with is the *Vocational Guidance Quarterly*, devoted almost entirely to vocational considerations. Two journals, one published by the American Psychological Association (APA), the *Journal of Counseling Psychology*, and one published by APA's Division 17, *The Counseling Psychologist*, devote much of their content to vocational behavior, but probably more counseling psychologists than school counselors read them regularly. In addition, some of the journals in vocational-technical education address guidance related issues, probably more so in recent issues than formerly.

All in all, it does appear that if a judgment were made as to the relative importance of vocationally oriented guidance practice solely on the basis of journal content, one would conclude that vocational guidance is not regarded as highly important. Whether this state of affairs is a cause or effect of the attention given to vocational matters is not the issue. Professional writings in these journals seem to support the impression that vocational guidance is not the first order of business for either contributors or subscribers.

Convention Programs

Another gauge of emphasis for a professional group can be the content of convention programs. Therefore, materials reflecting the content of recent national conventions of the American Personnel and Guidance Association (APGA) were reviewed. For the 1971 convention, the *Program Summaries and Abstracts* (APGA, 1971a) and *Research Reports* (APGA, 1971b) were used; for 1972, the printed convention program (APGA, 1972a) was used. As in the case of the journals, the examination was very superficial.

In the 1971 materials, 354 program summaries and 54 research reports were listed. Only 11.58 percent (41) of the programs and 24.07 percent (13) of the research reports had an obvious vocational focus. For 1972, the index for the convention program was consulted. There were 703 items indexed, 87 (12.38 percent) of which had a vocational focus. To be sure, these methods are not rigorous. As a result of cross-indexing, a single program may be listed more than once. Many programs may have been listed in ways that do not reveal their relevance. Furthermore, the title of a program or an index listing is not necessarily an accurate reflection of the program content. Other programs, which are truly relevant, may not be identified because key words do not appear in the title.

All of the limitations of the method notwithstanding, it does appear that a relatively small proportion of convention program effort is directed to vocational behavior. In fact, the proportion of programs that appear to be vocational is even considerably smaller than the proportion of APGA's membership that express interest in vocational guidance through membership in APGA's "vocational" division, the National Vocational Guidance Association (NVGA). Of APGA's 27,967 members as of August 1, 1972 (APGA, 1972b), 9,285 (33.53 percent) were members of NVGA. It may be that even though one-third of APGA's membership is interested enough in vocational guidance to join NVGA, those interests are met with considerably fewer than one-third of the convention programs.

Impact on Professionals

Three professional influences on counselor behavior were examined in this section. While the analysis of these forces was not thorough, the evidence supports the notion that attention to vocational guidance becomes obscured because of the many functions that counselors and other personnel specialists are concerned with. While there is no question that evidence drawn from titles of graduate courses, journal articles, and convention programs is superficial, it is the kind of evidence that is readily visible. Its very visibility makes it easily accessible to casual observers, and though it may be lamentable, casual observers make judgments about vocational guidance and the attention it gets from professionals. Some of those judgments have important ramifications. Beginning students make decisions which affect the course of their professional preparation. Teachers, administrators, and other school personnel draw conclusions about the relevance of what they think counselors contribute to school programs. Most important, perhaps, is that this kind of evidence can reinforce whatever tendencies already exist on the part of counselors to place less value on vocational guidance than on other areas of guidance. When they are on the job, it can be expected that they will devote more time to those activities they value highly. Because of the way this kind of valuing can influence task preferences at work and skill acquisitions, counselors are often best equipped to help students with those problems which are least directly related to work and employment.

The Humanness of Counselors

The extent to which vocational guidance is not a high priority in guidance practice is also a result of the kind of people that counselors are. Although counselors are often accused of establishing godlike expectations for themselves, they are human beings. They experience preferences, aspirations, desires, disappointments, limitations, and frustrations as all people do. Attributes of that character to be treated in this section are counselors' wishes to be helpful, to be credible, and to be successful.

On Being Helpful

Although they are a diverse group of people, by and large, counselors tend to have a strong social service orientation. Social service is defined by Kuder (1951) as "a preference for helping people." Kuder (1956) also estimated that counselors, as an occupational group, prefer to avoid conflict. This combination probably contributes to the tendency to offer whatever kind of help is requested. It is this tendency that seems influential in counselors' trying to do more than can be accomplished. When several groups hold out different expectations and counselors try to meet all of them, they give the appearance of trying to be all things to all people. The important point to make at this juncture is that counselors appear inclined to try to help in any way that is requested.

Probably the most common requests for help that counselors receive do not relate to future events. The young people with whom counselors work are likely to seek help with what is happening in their lives currently rather than what they anticipate in the future. Perhaps that is one of the reasons that counselors spend so much time on matters related to the management of students' daily lives: changing schedules, talking about relations with teachers or peers, making educational adjustments. Perhaps that is why most pre-college counseling occurs as deadlines for the submission of applications approach (or even after they have passed) or why most job-related counseling occurs during the last few weeks before graduation or dropping out of school.

Counselors are not concerned only with helping young people. They receive requests for assistance from adults with whom they interact, and they often report that they feel unprepared to help. Norris (1960) found that counselors wanted to improve their competencies in working with various adults. They wanted to help teachers to deal effectively with problem children. They wanted to be able to establish productive contacts with parents. They wanted to be able to identify and use community resources more effectively. They wanted to help teachers to develop instructional materials. And they wanted to conduct more effective research and evaluation. One proposed model for defining effective counselor performance (Lundquist and Chamley, 1971) actually went so far as to include counseling with teachers as a major component.

Perhaps this desire to help in so many ways is associated with the tendency so often observed in beginning counselors, the tendency to direct the lives of the people they work with, to make decisions for them. Although that tendency does diminish and counselors do become less directive with experience (Bohn, 1965), progress in that direction does not come easily. Clinical experience suggests that the major transition that occurs in becoming less directive is an emerging confidence that what is really helpful is quite different from what was originally so regarded. It seems that the *desire to be helpful does not change*, but *the definition of help does*.

Kuder (1956) has reported at least one study in which the social service interest of rehabilitation counselors was related to job satisfaction. In a study of job satisfaction in employment counselors (Bingham, 1969b), it was found that counselors see the help they provide to clients as an important source of job satisfaction. Those same counselors regarded other components of the job as sources of dissatisfaction. These findings are consistent with Hertzberg's (1959) hypothesis that job content is a source of satisfaction while the context in which the work occurs is a source of dissatisfaction. Neither of the studies cited involved school counselors, but similar data have been collected as an extension of this writer's study of employment counselors. Those data are still in process of analysis and cannot be reported at this time, but preliminary inspection indicates that the same tendency will be found in school counselors: they see contact which provides help for clients as a source of job satisfaction; they see contact with administrators and involvement in administrative procedures as sources of dissatisfaction. Is it possible that counselors, as a result of their desire to help, become involved in just as many job activities that are dissatisfying as are satisfying? If so, is this tendency more common early in their careers than later on? Does the same tendency vary with the level of directiveness observable in their counseling behavior? All of these questions are worthy of investigation by researchers in order to understand more fully how counselors use their "helping" orientation. Certainly they are questions that each counselor should ask himself from time to time.

Another series of questions counselors need to ask themselves concerns the proportion of effort directed to vocational guidance. Do counselors, in their eagerness to respond to presented problems of the moment, permit less apparent concerns to slip out of focus? Do they do enough to help clients keep the relationship between immediate difficulty and ultimate adjustment in useful perspective? Do they, in attempting to provide what is requested, fail to lend attention to other matters that might also be considered? Do they, in effect, permit vocational matters to be overlooked precisely because of attempts to be helpful?

On Being Credible

The growth of theoretical formulations related to guidance and the expansion of program offerings have made the work of the counselor very complex. The wide range of skills required to do what is expected of counselors makes the job very demanding. Because of these complexities and demands, it is not surprising that Falik and his associates (1971) observed that counselors try to oversimplify their lives. Yet they take on more complex job demands at the same time. They work on child study teams where interaction with other professionals can be intense. They attempt to influence developments in curriculum planning. They undertake some administrative functions. They study the community they work in as well as the children they guide. They perform, according to one analysis (Spears and others,

1961) as many as 40 distinct "jobs." The attempt to do so many different things may be one of the reasons it has become necessary, according to Brown (1971), to spend excessive amounts of time in defending what it is that counselors actually are. Certainly it is one of the reasons that led Falik and others (1971) to observe that counselors need to continue to remind themselves that service to children is the central purpose in their jobs, their *raison d'être*. Arguments may be advanced that all of the activities counselors engage in actually do offer service to children, but the involvement in them may overshadow the purpose, so the reminders are called for.

In addition to performing well all of the tasks encompassed by their many jobs, counselors are supposed to be objective about what they do. In particular, they are supposed to be nonjudgmental about their clients. They are taught to be accepting of all client behavior. It may be that the tendency to oversimplify cited above operates in this connection, too. While it is entirely in keeping with most counseling philosophies that counselors should not judge client behavior to be "good" or "bad," it is next to impossible to be nonjudgmental in all roles. But counselors sometimes act as if they expect that kind of thoroughness of themselves. Irrespective of the difficulty generated by such a demand, a question has been raised (Rousseve, 1971) as to whether it is appropriate to be nonjudgmental at all. In a society as complex as American society is, the impact on students of a non-judgmental role model needs to be considered. Counselors must question what purpose it serves to present to young people a model who has no opinions, who has no position on pressing social issues, who is essentially passive.

Effort to maintain a nonjudgmental posture will be fraught with difficulties. To begin with, to do so requires ability to live with strongly conflicting tendencies. Counselors are trained to be proficient in the use of evaluative instruments, i.e., to be effective evaluators, and then they are told not to evaluate. They are selected into preparation programs, in part, on the basis of verbal ability, and they are told to listen. As an occupational group, they prefer to be active in groups (Kuder, 1956), and they are told to assume passive roles. Though these implied restrictions on the application of skills or propensities is always situational to counseling *per se*, if counselors do attempt to assume the same posture in all the roles they play, then endless frustration could very well be encountered.

In addition, counselors' efforts to do more than they can must certainly reduce opportunities to do what they do well, what they prefer, and what they derive satisfaction from. As an illustration of this difficulty, interviewing will serve well. Kuder (1956) reported interviewing as one of the job activities which serves as a vehicle to express the preference to help. Satisfaction was seen to be related to helping activities. Therefore, it should be expected that counselors would spend major portions of their time doing tasks related to interviewing. Trotzer and Kassera (1971) cited professional opinion that would encourage them to do so. Roeber (1961) recommended that 50 percent of counselor time should be spent in individual contact with students. Strowig (1963) suggested that 40 percent should be given to actual counseling. Yet Trotzer and Kassera (1971) found that school counselors spend substantially less than half of their time in that kind of contact. For the counselors they studied only one-third of their time was spent counseling and only 14.8 percent of contact time with students was spent in vocational counseling. They also found that most counseling contacts dealt with educational concerns and that the longest counseling contacts were about personal problems. Interviews respecting vocational problems lasted an average of 26 minutes (substantially longer than often reported by counselors) and constituted less than 20 percent of the time actually spent counseling.

Thus, it appears that counselors spend relatively little time doing things related to their preferences and satisfactions. They want to be helpful, but they engage in some activities that leave them feeling helpless. In addition, there seems to be relatively little they can do about their situation. Control of their role functions, from a professional standpoint (according to Haettenschwiller, 1970), is in the hands of counselor educators, while control of the role functions in the practical sense is in the control of building principals. Under the circumstances, it would be understandable if they had feelings of incredibility about their own performance. It is little wonder that others sometimes see them as unbelievable. Furthermore, 80 percent of the time they spend in satisfying activity, and therefore, perhaps their most believable activity, is spent on problems related to educational and personal adjustment, rather than on vocational matters.

On Being Successful

In view of the prospects for frustration that occur in the daily lives of counselors, their desire to be perceived as successful may be especially keen. Personal experience certainly suggests that that is sometimes the case. In the extreme, the eagerness to feel successful may be associated with a search for working conditions in which success appears to be assured. One way to assure success in helping people is to concentrate on helping those who need little help. It has been charged, in fact (Ginzberg, 1967), that counselors generally render the greatest service to those of their clients who need the least help.

Evidence is lacking that the conclusion just reported has ever been investigated directly. At least one study has some bearing. On the proposition that "college-bound high school students and counselors have such similar value systems and subjective insights . . . the counselor can do little that the student cannot do, so far as college planning is concerned," Ford (1969) studied the decision-making behavior of school counselors, college-bound high school students, and noncollege-bound high school students. She found that all three groups had value systems which were essentially alike. In the case of the comparison between the counselors and college-bound students, she found that "both groups combined data in a similar fashion, both used similar subjective weights, both were consistent in their use of subjective weights and the groups did not differ in accuracy" (p. 36). In the case of the comparison between counselors and noncollege-bound students, they were different on all dimensions. She concluded that if counselors could be freed from advisement of college-bound students, the opportunities to work with students bound for noncollege level occupations would be limitless. These findings appear to lend support to the contention that counselors spend excessive time with those students who would reach the same decisions without help. The corollary, of course, is that employment-bound youth are neglected.

An alternative interpretation of Ford's data may be that counselors and college-bound students behave similarly because usable motivation has enabled the students to learn how to behave in the same productive ways that the counselors do. If that is so, then the challenge for counselors is a little different and two-fold. It is incumbent upon counselors to learn how to identify students' readiness to make decisions on their own and release them so more attention can be given to those who are still learning how. In addition, time should be spent to find effective ways to help noncollege-bound students to master appropriate decision-making skills.

An unrelated study casts a different light on counselor behavior respecting potential success of counselors. Using a unique design, Gold (1970) studied the effect of counselor-client dissimilarity on counselor judgment. She presented counselor trainees at four universities with transcripts of alleged applicants to "X State College" which was described by means of a freshman class profile. All of the transcripts reflected marginal academic achievement and low SAT scores. Half of the transcripts had a middle-class and half a lower-class father's occupation listed; equivalent transcripts were paired with the only difference being that one of each pair had a photograph of a white student attached, the second bore a photograph of a black student. No other reference was made to either socioeconomic status or race. After a lapse of three weeks, the transcripts were presented again with one difference: within each matched pair, the photographs were reversed. At each administration, the counselors were asked to respond to questions.

Respecting predictions of admission to and success in college, counselor behavior was inconsistent, so hypotheses that the counselors would favor applicants similar to themselves on those dimensions were not supported. Gold concluded that respondents may have been influenced by the fact that "new 'open' admissions programs and special programs for black and/or underprivileged students were becoming prevalent at the time of data collection" (pp. 155–156).

One finding, however, was relevant in the present context. In responding to a question about whether they would enjoy counseling the applicants, the counselors (all of whom were white and middle-class) behaved very consistently. They chose middle-class over lower-class applicants, white over black, and white middle-class over others. Even though the respondents did not behave decisively in predicting success for college applicants similar to themselves, they apparently preferred to establish counseling relationships with those who were.

The data of both the Ford and Gold studies must be interpreted with caution. Ford's work employed only actuarial data in the decision-making tasks, and Gold's permitted response to only a restricted number of specific questions. Modifications in either set of circumstances might very well produce different results. Interpreting the data at face value, however, would suggest that there is at least tentative support for the notion that counselors prefer to work with students who are similar to themselves not only in some demographic ways, but in terms of important behaviors as well. Proceeding to a further level of inference would suggest that they prefer to work with those whose life styles are similar to their own, that they are likely to be both more successful and more satisfied in working with college-bound students. Such tendencies could explain further why vocational considerations get less than sufficient attention from school counselors.

Summary

This chapter has reviewed several influences that appear to contribute to deemphasis of the vocational in guidance programs. Irrespective of program operators' intentions, these forces impinge in ways that make it difficult to keep vocational guidance foremost in guidance and personnel programs. Some of the factors identified are not calculated to make counselors happy. But they are phenomena that need to be brought into awareness so practitioners can examine their own contributions to the efficacy of guidance practices, and so investigators can formulate and test pertinent hypotheses. With the additional knowledge made available by those processes, it will be possible for functionaries who choose to emphasize vocational guidance to increase the probability that they will do so.

2

Vocational Maturity as Readiness for Employment

Theoretical formulations that adequately reflect the developmental nature of vocational behavior have been accumulating for more than two decades. The most elaborated system of such formulations is that of Super (1957, 1963, 1969), and his colleagues in the Career Pattern Study. Because vocational behavior is so complex, the models attempting to describe it are very complex. At least one critic (Carkhuff, 1968) has noted that it is difficult to tell how the "pieces" of Super's formulation fit together. When pieces which were generated in different places are brought into a single system, they may fit together even less well. A comprehensive framework, reflecting all available knowledge, is not easy to accommodate into the busy schedules of school personnel as they attempt to look at their roles in relation to youth employment. Attention to all of the components of vocational development is so demanding that practitioners may be discouraged from trying to make practical applications of what they do know in their work settings. On the surface at least, it appears that there is much more needed than they can possibly do. In recognition of that kind of eventuality, the present chapter will be confined to a discussion of some components of vocational maturity. Somewhat detailed attention will be given to planfulness and briefer remarks will be offered on occupational information, motivation to work, and readiness for employment.

Vocational Maturity

Super and Overstreet (1960) postulated a developmental frame of reference for the study of vocational maturity. They placed importance on *developmental tasks* defined as "a task which arises at or about a certain period in the life of the individual, successful achievement of which leads to his happiness and to success with later tasks, while failure leads to unhappiness in the individual, disapproval by society, and difficulty with later tasks." (Havighurst, 1953, p. 2). They argued that the study of vocational maturity is important because, in effect, it can be viewed as the study of readiness to learn about vocational behavior. Thus, it would be useful to be able to ascertain an individual's vocational maturity (i.e., his readiness to proceed to higher-level developmental tasks) in junior and senior high school so that appropriate activities and experiences could be planned to facilitate his development toward adequate vocational adjustment.

Super and Overstreet studied 27 indices of vocational maturity in ninth-grade boys in Middletown, New York. Their analysis yielded five factors of vocational maturity. Although those factors accounted for only 38 percent of the variance, the investigators expressed confidence that if the reliability of the instruments could be increased, then a larger proportion of the variance could be accounted for. One factor which they named *planning orientation*, was clearly superior to the others in that it was important to all four of the "adequate" indices of vocational maturity: (1) concern with choice; (2) acceptance of responsibility for choice and planning; (3) specificity of information about preferred occupations; and (4) specificity of planning for preferred occupations. Actually, the influence of that planning orientation factor was so convincing that they concluded "it (vocational maturity) is, essentially, planfulness." (p. 150). Experimentation over the years has not altered that opinion substantially; planfulness continues to be the central component of vocational maturity (Super and Forrest, 1972; Super and Jordaan, 1972).

Planfulness

Attending only to planfulness at this point is not to be construed to mean that other components of vocational maturity are unimportant. Some of them appear more important in recent analyses (Jordaan, 1972) than they did earlier. One purpose for the present limited focus is to highlight the centrality of planning; another is to suggest that people who work in schools (and in other educational settings, for that matter) can help young people become effective planners. An assumption basic to this discussion is that people learn how to plan. If that assumption is accurate, then schools should play an important part in facilitating that learning. Consequently, the subject warrants careful consideration in relation to how school personnel meet their responsibilities bearing on the employment of youth.

Before proceeding to a discussion of planning, however, it is in order to make an important observation about theorizing and research in vocational development. The formulation of theory related to vocational development has been based largely on data related to upper-middle-class white males who are planning to go to or are currently in college. As a consequence, not nearly enough is known about the behavior of young people who are different from that group. The need for further investigation respecting the effects of socioeconomic status on vocational development has been pointed out a number of times (e.g., Holland, 1969; Bingham, 1969a).

LoCascio (1964) has criticized prevailing theory in vocational development on the grounds that it is based on the assumption that development for all individuals is continuous. He argued that such a proposition is misleading and erroneous, that, as a matter of fact, for some people vocational development is delayed and for others it is impaired. Elaboration of LoCascio's formulation respecting continuous, delayed, and impaired development has been presented elsewhere (Bingham, 1967). A detailed examination of planning readiness as it is related to his position is relevant to the present discussion.

Looking at planfulness in the context of the developmental framework proposed by Super and Overstreet raises some interesting questions about the readiness of individuals to learn planning as a developmental task while proceeding toward vocational maturity. One of the characteristics of developmental tasks is that their accomplishment is expected more or less uniformly for all individuals at the same time. The classical instance of such an expectation is the imposition of the first grade upon children at six years of age (Anderson, 1957). It would be useful to examine the imposition of the first grade on six-year-olds as a developmental task, particularly with respect to readiness to learn planning behavior.

Doubtless, ability to learn to plan is affected by a variety of factors such as aptitude, personality, and interest, but nobody starts out at a higher level of skill than someone else. Vocational maturity, in general, is related to intelligence (Crites, 1969a), so planning ability probably is, too. But in the beginning, there are probably greater differences in social opportunities to accumulate planning skills than in other variables. People who experience differential opportunities to witness and participate in planning activities during the preschool years will enter school at differing levels of readiness to learn planning behaviors. Unless something is done to reduce those differences, it seems reasonable to anticipate that they will increase as children progress through the grades.

Continuous Development

A young person who has grown up in a family of professional people can find in his daily experience considerable evidence that people plan well. He also learns that the planning has a payoff. Such a person has probably had many opportunities to participate with his family in making plans about a variety of things: purchasing new clothing, going on vacation, buying a new car, etc. Furthermore, he has probably overheard a variety of conversations among his parents and other adults involving planning in which he is not allowed to participate directly. The latter category may have included such things as buying a house, refinancing a home mortgage, making investments in stocks or bonds, buying life insurance, putting money aside for children's college expenses, paying into a pension fund, and making plans for retirement.

Under the kind of circumstances just described, it is entirely likely that children could learn that a significant effect of planfulness is that certain events tend to happen on a more or less regular schedule. For example, father dependably brings home a paycheck at regular intervals, important family activities such as mealtime and bedtime occur when they are planned, and special events such as parties, picnics, and other gatherings happen when participants expect them to happen.

They learn indirectly that in business activities, as well as in social events, people make appointments and arrive at the same place to meet together at more or less the same time. They may discover, by participation or hearsay that planning for social as well as business occasions may include some expectation as to what is going to happen, that is, an agenda is conceived.

An important outcome of early experience in and observation of successful planning is the emergence of positive attitudes about planning. Expectations become crystallized that planned events happen as scheduled. Assurance develops that one can plan (and therefore predict) his own behavior. Such conviction opens the door to possibilities that other things can be predicted. The future can be faced with certainty.

Delayed Development

Those young people who experience delayed development encounter quite a different sequence of experiences in their early life. Daily routine may expose them to only limited evidence that people plan well. Most planning is probably of a relatively short-range character. Even when there are plans, they may not work out. Planning for activities such as buying a car or providing for college may be absent or minimal. Decisions about some important purchases are probably made impulsively as money becomes available. Income may not be regular enough to permit long-range saving even if family members have adequate planning skills. Large purchases are likely to be made on the installment plan. A young observer may learn, more than anything else, that due dates have a way of materializing unexpectedly.

Developing a sense of control over one's daily schedule is much less likely than in the case of the continuous developer. A daily routine may be present, but irregularities may be characteristic. Paychecks may be fairly regular but less than adequate. Mealtime may not be entirely dependable: one or another child may have to run to the local grocery at the last minute to get something for dinner. Planning may not occur early enough to assure that supplies and materials are conveniently available when needed. Family gatherings may be impulsively organized and planned only over the short run.

Growing up in circumstances of delayed development may lead to expectations that punctuality is something imposed by some outside force. Getting to work on time is what the boss requires. Tardiness at school leads to detention. Movies and football games may start on time, buses may run on schedule, and the supermarket closes at 9:30. But they are all under the control of someone else.

Attitudes about planning are likely to be mixed. Sometimes planned events turn out as intended; sometimes they do not. While there is likely to be knowledge that a reasonable plan is attainable, more often it is within the grasp of another person's skill than one's own. The future is not necessarily threatening, but it is chancey. It is safer not to think too far ahead.

Impaired Development

The range of experiences encountered by the impaired developer is quite different from that of either of the others. He may witness very limited, if any, evidence of planning by adults in his immediate environment. If there is any planning, he does not participate in it and may seldom have an opportunity to observe it. Lack of understanding of planfulness provides no basis for anticipating a beneficial outcome. If events just happen, what is there to do about it.

Whatever routine there is in the daily schedule is probably minimal. Income may be irregular causing other activities dependent on income to be irregular, too. When money is available, it may be spent with little regard to priority of need. Instead of planning, there may be considerable talking about planning. Such discussion almost never leads to action. In the extreme, it is akin to Jeeter Lester's almost daily self-admonition: "Yep, tomorrow, I just gotta plow that north 40."

By contrast to continuous and delayed developers, the child whose development has been impaired has little or no sense of the future. It would be nice to plan, perhaps, but why bother. Plans never materialize, anyway.

If youngsters from all three of these developmental patterns have the first grade thrust upon them at the same time, it is essentially impossible that their responses will be equally fruitful. They are differentially prepared to meet teachers' expectations in terms of readiness for planning. The simplest planning expectations will be met well by the continuous developers, haltingly by the delayed developers, and perhaps not at all by the impaired developers. As the succeeders gain the rewards and the nonsucceeders do not, the gaps between them in readiness for the next developmental task will widen. Success will lead to confidence of more success, and continuing failure will lead to despair. Irrespective of the increasing differences in readiness, expectations for mastery of developmental tasks will remain uniform.

Gribbons and Lohnes (1968) have studied what they called Readiness for Vocational Planning. Scores on their scale increased from grades 8–10 supporting the developmental nature of the construct. The overlapping they found between grades 8 and 10 indicated that some 8th graders are more advanced in readiness for vocational planning than 10th graders are. Thompson (1972) also reported that planning behavior increases with age.

Time Orientation

Time orientation is consistently related to vocational maturity (Super and Overstreet, 1960; Jordaan, 1972). High scorers on vocational maturity indices tend to be future oriented, and lower scorers tend not to be. In oversimplified terms low scorers are oriented to immediate choices, moderate scorers to short- and intermediate-range choices, and high scorers to long-range choices. While direct application of these data to situations similar to those described in the discussion of LoCascio's formulation would be inappropriate, some interesting analogies are possible. The vocational maturity data cited apply to adolescents and young adults while the illustrations described are of preschoolers. The data and illustrations represent readiness at different points in the developmental process. If the described differences in early development were present at the junior high school level, they could be translated into measurable vocational maturity differences.

In the illustration used to describe impaired development above, there appears to be some evidence of awareness of the need to plan. Such awareness is viewed as an index of vocational maturity. In the illustrative case, that awareness leads to no productive activity; it seems to be the final step in the process. Because of the inaction, it represents a very low level of vocational maturity. In the case of the delayed developer, the manifest behavior appears to be related to indices associated with immediate choices, and perhaps some awareness that longer-range planning is needed. The continuous developer showed not only awareness of the need for immediate choices but for intermediate and ultimate choices as well. There is also evidence of acceptance of responsibility for those choices and plans. Thus, in using these early-life analogies, it appears that continuous developers manifest more sophisticated readiness to deal with planfulness than either of the others, and that impaired developers manifest less of that readiness than delayed developers.

Socioeconomic Status

Intuitively, one would expect a substantial relationship between continuity of development and socioeconomic status. In the Super and Overstreet (1960) study, there was little evidence to support such a notion. Almost none of the indices they employed was related to socioeconomic status. Occupation of the subject's father was a notable exception. In later analysis, using the same boys and identical measures (Super, 1972), a number of fair to moderate correlations between socioeconomic indicators and vocational maturity were found. Apparently, socioeconomic differences have increasing impact on vocational maturity with age. However, another study (Gribbons and Lohnes, 1968) found no relationship between vocational maturity and socioeconomic status. The relationship between socioeconomic level and continuity of development needs careful investigation.

Even if the relationship just discussed does exist, that is, that opportunities to experience continuous rather than delayed or impaired vocational development are a function of socioeconomic status, it is surely not absolute. Other factors must affect those differences in opportunity as well. If two people have equal planning skills, the one with higher income probably finds long-range planning more manageable. One need not search far in personal experience, however, to identify someone of sufficient economic resources who is a poor planner.

Obviously the relationship is a complex one, but it does seem that LoCascio's proposition has some merit for conceptualizing differences in development. Developmental differences are important to school personnel because they represent differences in readiness to cope with expectations. If school programs are to maximize the effect they have on the readiness of *all* youth to cope with demands of employment, they are going to have to set expectations that differentially address unequal levels of student readiness.

Occupational Information

The major offering of the educational enterprise is information. Much of learning, as it is typically handled in schools, is the accumulation of knowledge. The assumption is that the accumulated knowledge will one day be utilized to facilitate individual adjustment.

In a parallel sense to that discussed in the previous section, there are probably developmental differences among students in readiness both to accumulate and to use information. By extrapolation, it can be seen that those differences apply to readiness to make an adequate adjustment.

The possession of information about occupations has been a consistent correlate of vocational maturity. More mature subjects are better informed (Super and Overstreet, 1960). Other relationships have been reported by Super (1972). Specificity of information about preferred occupations tends to increase with age and experience. So does knowledge about the conditions of work, opportunities for advancement, and supply and demand. Store of occupational information in 9th grade was related to vocational success in young adulthood. Information about training and education required for preferred occupations is moderately related to level of attainment at age 25. The expected relationship that Super reported, that 12th graders consider fewer occupations than 9th graders, might be interpreted as evidence of increasing self-knowledge.

The importance of information to not only the present but also the ultimate vocational behavior of youth is evident. Opportunities made available in schools for young people to accumulate and use information have an important influence on their behavior. Presumably, the manner of presentation interacts with readiness in ways that affect the outcomes of those offerings.

It is important that schools make occupational and educational information available to students, but the information needs to be in a form that students can use. Those who make information available need to be cognizant that not all students are equally prepared to make effective use of information which is presented only in cognitive and abstract terms. Some students learn more by observing job activities directly than by reading about them. Others learn best by actual participation. School programs which take information dissemination seriously will have a wide range of offerings with variety available in form of presentation as well as in content. *The most successful programs are those in which particularized decisions are made as to student readiness in terms of both content and style of presentation.*

Motivation to Work

Motivation to work has not been studied directly in the context of vocational maturity. However, motivation is a complex construct, and some of the variables discussed in the vocational maturity literature appear to be related to it. Crites (1969a) conceptualizes several vocational choice competencies which may be affected by motivation to work: goal selection, self-knowledge, problem solving. His "involvement" as a vocational choice attitude may also be related. Super's (1972) use of "commitment" in describing exploratory and establishment behavior appears not to be unrelated to motivation. Level of aspiration, reported by Jordaan (1972), appears in a number of formulations of motivation. Regnancy (Super and others, 1963) is explicitly related to motivation. Motivation to work can also be expected to increase with age through adolescence. The finding that 80 percent of the subjects in the Career Pattern Study (Super, 1972) were engaging in positive, stabilizing coping behaviors at age 25 may be, at least in part, a function of motivation growing out of increasing family responsibilities. Over all, the construct of motivation to work should be of interest to anyone concerned with the vocational maturity of young people, especially where that concern is related to employment.

Motivation to work has been studied in another context of interest in relation to the employment of youth. Indik (1966a) thought his formulation would be of interest to personnel workers because they often try to assess motivation to work in making hiring decisions. Although the purposes are quite different, that formulation may be of interest as well to workers concerned with the facilitation of vocational maturity.

Indik based his formulation of motivation to work on Atkinson's (1964) principle that motivation to succeed is associated with two situational components: expectancy to succeed and incentive value of success. He considered the converse of each of those elements, leading to a six-part formulation. Thus, *Motivation to Work* is conceived of as the product of *Motive to Work* times *Expectancy to Work* times *Incentive to Work*. *Motivation to Avoid Work* is also a product: *Motive to Avoid Work* times *Expectancy to Avoid Work* times *Incentive to Avoid Work*. An overall score called *Residual Behavior Potential to Work* is obtained by subtracting *Motivation to Avoid Work* from *Motivation to Work*. Scores are obtained by means of a 36-item questionnaire including a six-item scale for each component.

In terms of construct validity, Indik found several supportive results: males score higher than females; no difference was associated with race; subjects with more dependents score higher than those with fewer dependents; there was a negative relationship between score and number of months unemployed; and there was no significant relationship between score and age, but there was a trend in the expected direction. In connection with the last observation it must be noted that all subjects were over 22 years old and registered with a state employment service. A sample including younger subjects and representing a broader range of occupational levels could be expected to yield a positive and significant relationship to age.

In a study of 100 Manpower Development and Training ACT (MDTA) enrollees, 170 MDTA applicants, and 230 controls (Indik, 1966b), the *Motive to Work* and *Motive to Avoid Work Scales* produced more impressive results than the others. Those subjects in the labor force scored higher on *Motive to Work* and lower on *Motive to Avoid Work* than those not in the labor force. In another study (Indik and Seymore, 1969) of 40 enrollees in a community action training program it was found that those who remained in the training program seven or more months had higher average scores than those who withdrew earlier. There was no clear evidence that the training program had a consistent effect on motivation to work, but only 13 enrollees were examined in that connection.

All of the investigations reported by Indik were conducted in settings other than schools, and for the most part, with people beyond school age. Therefore, the results are not directly applicable to school children. The idea of measuring motivation to work, though, is of interest to school people. That may be particularly so in as much as the subjects in these studies were like those with whom schools are often not very successful. It may be possible to enhance motivation to work by providing stimulating, relevant, and satisfying prework experiences in educational and training settings. As Indik (1966a) pointed out, such measurement can be expected to account for some of the variance in predicting occupational status, but must be regarded as a single variable among a number used for the same purpose. It may be useful to investigate the possibility of measuring differential motivation to work in specific occupations or jobs.

Readiness for Employment

That vocational maturity is a developmental phenomenon which increases with age is well documented (Super and Jordaan, 1972). Those who are vocationally mature are readier for employment than those who are immature. There is considerable evidence that young people proceed through high school with substantial differences in readiness to cope with the vocationally relevant developmental tasks they encounter. In spite of those differences, all ninth graders are required to plan a high school program of studies and all twelfth graders are expected to make and execute post high school plans. Whether they are ready to do so or not, at more or less the same time in their chronological development, all students have to make a range of vocationally relevant choices.

As young people progress through junior and senior high school, their readiness to cope with employment-related activities in their lives increases. Such readiness needs to be viewed as relative, however. The fact that increase occurs does not necessarily mean that adequacy to meet institutional expectations has emerged. On the contrary, available evidence indicates that in many ways it has not.

A number of the findings of the Career Pattern Study (Super, 1972) contain evidence of developmental progress toward adequacy of readiness: independence of work experience increased, preferences became more specific, both degree of commitment and consistency of choice were higher in twelfth grade than in ninth. On the other hand, the data clearly indicate a lack of readiness to live up to some important expectations respecting choice. Only 16 percent of the twelfth graders had the same specific occupational preference they had in ninth grade. Others had changed field, or level, or both. More than 68 percent of them had minimal commitment to their occupational preferences. More than half of the position changes of boys studied were rated as aimless. One would interpret the data about vocational maturity as indicating that, for the most part, by the time young people reach the early or mid-twenties, they are manifesting the kind of vocational behavior generally expected of them at some time in secondary school. Many of them are clearly not ready for the kind of decision-making tasks they must face in school. Jordaan (1972) has offered a tentative description of the kind of high school student who is likely to have achieved success and satisfaction in work by the age of 25:

> He comes from a middle rather than from a lower class home, gets good grades, is active in school activities, has hobbies and pastimes which he pursues out of school, has worked after school, has goals which are in keeping with his intellectual level and has a good deal of information about the occupation which he thinks he might follow. In short, he is a doer; he is active and involved both in school and out of school and is not only engaging his environment but exploring it.

Super's recent (1972) conclusion appears to be justified: vocational development in grades 8, 9, and 10 has progressed to the point where vocational guidance activities can be made meaningful, but it has not progressed far enough to justify directional decision making. Even at the twelfth-grade level, "there appears to be only a limited basis for sound directional vocational decision-making in the majority of students" (p. 12).

Summary

This chapter has examined some of the components of vocational maturity and considered them in relation to the expectation that young people must face, particularly in schools, as they develop. Readiness to cope with developmental tasks is regarded as central to vocational maturity. In that context, planfulness, occupational information, motivation to work, and readiness for employment were discussed. On the basis of the evidence reviewed, it was concluded that most adolescents are not adequately prepared to meet the vocationally relevant demands they encounter in school.

3

Self-Perceptions and Employment

Any attempt to understand young people's behavior in relation to employment must address considerable attention to the way in which they perceive themselves. Self-perception is widely accepted as an important determinant of behavior. Some writers (e.g., Snygg and Combs, 1949; and Kelly, 1955) have built elaborate theories around the relationship between self-perception and behavior in general, but few have been systematic in developing formulations specifically about relationships between self-perception and vocational behavior. An early and very significant effort to address that relationship systematically is Super's (1951, 1953) hypothesis that occupational choice is an effort to implement self-concepts. He later elaborated it in considerable detail (1957) and developed important efforts to translate it into operational terms (1963a & b). His formulation is particularly relevant in the present context because it has been investigated in view of the knowledge gained in the Career Pattern Study research.

Self Concept Theory

Super's theory (Super and Bohn, 1970) recognizes a number of influences, internal and external to the individual, that affect career behavior. In that view, the individual weighs factors and chooses among alternatives. The "choosing person" theory is favored over the "accident" theory advanced by some sociologists as the central determinant of specific behaviors. It is postulated that the choosing person plays a synthesizing role in determining specific behaviors executed generally within the broad limits established by socioeconomic and physical factors.

Self-concept theory recognizes three aspects of self-concept development: formation of self concepts, translation of them into occupational terms, and self implementation through active involvement in occupational tasks.

Self-concept theory recognizes three aspects of self-concept develop- self and environment and by differentiation of self from others. In this process, the individual accumulates a large number of impressions of himself, his interests and abilities. He, in effect, collects considerable data about himself. He plays a variety of roles and tries out new behaviors. He tests his perceived attributes in different situations, and discovers which behaviors lead to satisfaction and a sense of achievement. Some roles he plays have general meaning for him, some have situational meaning, as in the case of those seen as relevant to occupational endeavors. Evaluations of performance in various roles and judgments about preferences lead to crystallization and clarification of self-perceptions.

"The translation of self concepts into occupational terms takes place through one or more of three processes: identification, experience, and observation" (Super and Bohn, 1970, p. 148). Identification is a generalized attempt to be like an admired adult without considering specific traits. Experience resulting from circumstances permits discovery of unsuspected talents or interests. Observation enables an individual to learn that some of his attributes are important in certain occupations.

Implementation of occupational self concepts is characterized by action. The individual transforms a self concept into a reality by finding a job or obtaining the education or training needed to qualify for an occupation. As he progresses in a chosen occupation, his self-perceptions may be modified. Preservation of self concepts occurs as the individual tries to hold his own in advancing age, and self-concept adjustment occurs as he copes with the dramatic changes in status and circumstances associated with retirement.

As an individual engages in any kind of behavior, he gains impressions of all aspects of himself. Through processes such as generalization and abstraction, the individual relates these impressions one to another, ascribes meaning to them, and organizes them into self concepts. Meanings are usually ascribed to self in the context of some role. Thus, a self concept is an image of the self performing a set of functions or engaging in a set of relationships.

Measurement of Occupational Self Concepts

Various aspects of self concepts have been related to participation in and preparation for occupational roles. For example, Fitts (1972b) reported that rehabilitation patients consistently manifest relationships between self concepts and persistence in training. He also reported that dropouts from paratrooper training in the Israeli army have lower self-esteem and more difficulty with self-definition than persisters. Ekman and his colleagues (1962) concluded that the observed increase in feelings of self-importance during basic military training was associated with an increased sense of competence. Korman (1967) found self-esteem to be a moderator of the relationship between self-perceived abilities and vocational choice.

Self Concepts and Occupational Concepts

An important test of the efficacy of a theoretical formulation is the kind of investigation it produces. A theory which generates viable hypotheses holds the potential to make significant advances in knowledge. Although efforts to measure self concepts have sometimes led to inconsistent and inconclusive observations, when the related variable has been the individual's concept of the occupation, hypotheses derived from self-concept theory have generally been supported. In that sense, Super's theory has been efficacious.

Similarity between self concepts and occupational concepts has been the subject of a number of investigations. It has generally been hypothesized that there is greater agreement between self concepts and occupational concepts in relation to preferred occupations than in those which are not preferred. In studying relationships among self-descriptions, occupational stereotypes, and vocational preference Blocher and Shutz (1961) found that twelfth-grade boys perceived greater similarity between self and stereotypes of workers in high-interest occupations than between self and workers in low-interest occupations. Englander (1960) was able to distinguish among undergraduate majors by comparing self-descriptions and occupational role descriptions. Warren (1961) concluded that college students tend to change to majors related to occupations for which role and self-descriptions were congruent. Stephenson (1961) found that non-admitted medical school applicants persist in seeking occupational roles related to medicine.

The Translation Model

A model for investigating the translation of self concepts into occupational terms has been recommended by Starishevsky and Matlin (1963). Based on their model, they developed the Modified Rep Test which is an adaptation of Kelly's (1955) Role Construct Repertory Test incorporating some features of Osgood's (1957) Semantic Differential. The technique permits subjects to generate personal constructs which are then used to rate self and occupational roles. An occupational self concept is reflected in agreement between self concept and a particular occupational concept, which they called level of incorporation. Several investigations have employed this model or variations of it.

Oppenheimer (1964) studied the relationship between self concepts and ratings of preferred and nonpreferred occupations. Of 81 liberal arts undergraduate men, 60 rated themselves as more similar to preferred occupations, nine as more similar to nonpreferred occupations, and 12 were tied. He also concluded that self-esteem is related to similarity between self concepts and occupational preferences.

Shiner (1963) investigated the relationship between self concept and change of occupation in 32 former teachers training to become counselors. He found significantly higher agreement between self concept and concept of the selected occupation than between self concept and concept of the occupation being left.

In an extension of the Shiner study (Bingham, 1966), it was found that 82 full-time graduate students making the same occupational change, from teacher to counselor, manifested more similarity between self and chosen occupation than between self and relinquished occupation. They also scored better in that connection than controls (44 employed teachers with no plans to become counselors). The expected increase in similarity between self and counselor descriptions over the course of training did not materialize.

Rampel (1967) studied the self concepts of college-educated women interested in returning to the labor force. Alumnae of a mathematics retraining program, trainees in the program, and housewives who had expressed interest but had not enrolled were tested. She found general support for the hypothesis that self concepts are more similar to occupational concepts for the chosen occupation than for the relinquished occupation. In this case, the relinquished occupation was homemaking.

In a study of the effects of student teaching on the occupational self concepts of prospective teachers, Grundfest (1970) found that teacher trainees saw greater similarity between themselves and the role of "teacher" than "dietician." Because she found no support for the hypothesis that agreement between self and role concepts increases more during student teaching than during other aspects of professional preparation, Grundfest concluded that commitment to teaching crystallized before entry into the training program. Her data suggest that change in self concept is difficult to measure over a short period of time.

Siggers (1971) studied the occupational self concepts of 40 established counselors and 40 counseling interns. Although their levels of incorporation for the occupation of counselor were significantly different from each other, they were similar in important respects. For both groups, the level of incorporation was higher for the preferred occupation (counselor) than for others. It was higher for nonpreferred but related occupations (teacher and social worker) than for a nonpreferred and unrelated occupation (lawyer).

Metadimensions of Self Concepts

"The dimensions of the self concept which must be studied . . . are clearly the dimensions of personality, the traits that people attribute to others and to themselves" (Super, 1963b, p. 19). When traits are identified by means of self report, as Wylie (1961) indicated as appropriate, the content of self-descriptions varies from one person to another. This fact complicates efforts to compare individuals. To facilitate such comparison, traits can be studied to determine what they have in common despite their differing content. These characteristics of the traits that people attribute to themselves are, in effect, dimensions of the dimensions, or what Super (1963b) has called the *metadimensions* of self concepts. Metadimensions identified by Super include: self-esteem, clarity, abstraction, realism, certainty, stability, refinement, scope, structure, idiosyncrasy, harmony, flexibility, and regnancy.

Miner (1963), in a review of criticisms of self-concept research, concluded that the metadimensional approach affords "the most provocative and intuitively appealing means of studying self concepts" (p. 43). Simply the prospect of making comparisons among apparently different self-reported attributes is appealing. Perplexing investigational problems may become manageable with this kind of formulation. Just as it is possible for people to judge paintings in terms of color, texture, or perspective, rather than content, or to evaluate music in terms of rhythm or harmony instead of content, it is becoming possible to analyze people's self reports irrespective of specific content.

Some of the studies mentioned in the previous section included examination of one or more metadimensions as part of their focus. Several others are reported by Super and Jordaan (1972). In general these investigations have established relations between some of the metadimensions and behavioral criteria. The work to date is promising, but some of the procedures need refinement to improve efficiency, and existing gaps in conceptualization need to be filled. Much remains to be done to gain fuller understanding of how people use work to translate self-perceptions into expression.

Translation of Self Concepts into Occupational Terms

Since the present monograph is concerned primarily with the relationship between self-perception and preparation for employment, the primary focus in terms of self-concept development is on the translation of self concepts into vocational terms. A major portion of the behavior and conceptualization associated with translation occurs during adolescence. Thus, much school-based experience can be relevant to the processes of translation.

Processes of Translation

As indicated above, Super views the translation of self concepts into occupational terms as occurring through one or more of three processes: identification, experience, observation. The present focus demands a more careful look at those processes.

Identification

Identification is a generalized process reflecting an arbitrary desire to be like an admired adult, usually without consideration of particular attributes. As identification with more than one role model occurs, differences in their traits may be brought into specific focus. The individual's evaluation of which characteristics are probably compatible with his own aspirations (i.e., what he wants to become) leads to more or less conscious effort to explore them more fully in direct application. While identification begins as a global, arbitrary wish to be like someone else, specific traits are gradually brought into awareness and examined in some situational contexts.

Experience

Experience in a role serves to facilitate translation of self concepts into occupational terms. Early experience probably occurs most often as a result of circumstances beyond the individual's control. Some opportunities for experience may be essentially accidental, some may be coincidental to other events, and some may be imposed by others. As development proceeds and the individual matures, experience is probably more and more frequently chosen. With maturity, an increasing proportion of such experience can be expected to be deliberately planned. Sophisticated individuals plan experience specifically to test certain self-perceptions.

Observation

Translation of self concepts into occupational terms also occurs by observation. All individuals have some opportunities to observe adults at work from early childhood. Even casual attention provides important information about working conditions, required abilities or interests, and possibilities for satisfaction. Overhearing adults talking about their jobs is another source of information. Intentional discussion with selected workers can provide additional knowledge. Reading, growing incidentally or planfully out of free-time activity or school assignments, can spark interests or suggest avenues of exploration of self-perceptions. As the individual matures, his observations can be expected to become increasingly self-directed and purposeful.

Restatement of Translation Processes

On the basis of the foregoing discussion, it can be seen that translation of self concepts into occupational terms can begin through any one of the processes recognized by Super. The beginning point may be a global and arbitrary identification, an incidental experience, or a casual observation. The nature of the translation process, however, seems to be that the impact of behavior on self-perceptions is gradually brought into focus, and increasingly specific judgments are made as to preferences for the application of certain attributes in particular situations. More or less consciously, new experiences are initiated and emerging self-perceptions are modified and/or clarified. With increasing awareness as to purpose, new opportunities, direct or vicarious, to observe people at work are sought, and comparisons between one's own attributes and situational requirements are made.

While initial steps toward translation may be global and arbitrary, the maturing individual manifests increasingly specific and deliberate efforts to translate his meaning of self into occupational terms. He "tries on" many attributes in various situations and more or less consciously decides to retain some, discard others, and modify still others. The large possible number of combinations of events in this process offers opportunities for each individual to pursue and define his own essential uniqueness.

A refinement of Super's formulation seems possible. Translation of self concepts into occupational terms begins with one of the recognized processes: identification, experience, observation. For most people, all three operate. As the individual develops toward maturity, his efforts at translation become more selective, purposeful, and focused. A sophisticated individual actively seeks opportunities to learn how he functions in particular situations. Translation begins as an arbitrary, global, and casual activity, but, ideally, as implementation nears, it becomes reasoned, particularized, and planned. *Potential for self-actualization in an occupation is characterized by the kind of accurate self-awareness that results from productive translation of self-perceptions into occupational terms.*

Translation in Schools

As shown above, self concepts have consistently been demonstrated to be related to occupational choice. By extension of the theory, even though specific empirical data are limited, it can be argued that self concepts are also related to behaviors relevant to choice of occupation but which usually occur earlier in people's lives. By and large, when investigation of such phenomena has been conducted in schools, the focus has usually been the high school years, and appropriately so. The landmark study of this type is the Career Pattern Study (Super and others, 1957) which not only followed subjects through high school, but into adulthood as well. A major finding of that study is that high school students are generally not ready to make the vocationally relevant decisions demanded of them. Given that finding, two alternative courses of action seem clear: (1) the decisions could be delayed until higher levels of readiness are present; or (2) concerted effort could be directed to acceleration of the developmental processes affecting readiness.

Schools (and other forces in society) seem ill-disposed toward postponement of the decision-making demands. Many educational programs, at high school and post-high school levels, have specific occupational orientations. Eligibility for entry into many of them is determined in some measure by high school curricular choices. Voluntary termination of formal education, typically, can occur at age 16. Most adolescents who are disposed to drop out of school will be seeking jobs immediately after doing so irrespective of their vocational maturity.

The extent to which it is possible to accelerate processes related to the translation of self concepts is unknown. Empirical data about related behavior before the high school years is limited for good reason. Much of the vocationally-related behavior that young people engage in is based in fantasy, making it very difficult to observe and to interpret. In addition, self-concept data are particularly difficult to collect because self-perceptions are emerging and not entirely crystallized. Young people may have difficulty reporting what they understand well; not many understand their self concepts fully. It is easy to agree that schools should attempt to facilitate readiness for translation of self concepts, but present knowledge permits more comfortable judgments about desirable outcomes of those efforts than about suitable times or methods of beginning them.

Knowledge that the information one has about occupations is related to vocational maturity has led some functionaries to recommend the introduction of occupational information into the school curriculum earlier than has been customary. Widespread application of that recommendation may be premature. Since little is known about readiness to use information effectively, it would be wise to make information available to limited groups of younger students while readiness to use it is studied carefully. Results could then be used to make modifications in existing practices.

One study has specifically examined the effect of different high school programs on translation of self concepts into occupational terms. Wertheim (1971) reasoned that participation in education definitely geared toward employment in particular occupations would be associated with greater translation of self concepts into occupational terms than participation in more general education.

From that reasoning, she hypothesized that boys enrolled in vocational-technical high schools achieve higher level of incorporation scores than boys in either general or vocational-technical programs in comprehensive high schools. The hypothesis was supported for the twelfth graders she tested: 31 vocational-technical students manifested higher levels of incorporation between self and anticipated entry occupation then either of the others. No difference was found between the 30 vocational-technical and 15 general students attending the comprehensive high school. Since no differences were observed among ninth-grade comparison groups, she concluded that the observed difference among twelfth-graders was a function of the different educational *experience*. No doubt, there were also better opportunities for both *identification* and *observation* available to the vocational-technical school boys than to the others.

A finding not included in Wertheim's original report[1] is of interest in the present context. All three groups of boys manifested significantly lower levels of incorporation for a rejected occupation than for others studied. It is particularly notable that for both groups of boys in the comprehensive high school this was the only difference observed among their occupational self concepts. The fact that all of the boys had differentiable self concepts for nonpreferred occupations, and

---

[1] Personal communication, September, 1972.

some of them for only the nonpreferred occupation, suggests that translation of self concepts may occur first in negative terms. This conclusion would be consistent with findings in research on vocational interests that "dislikes" crystallize earlier than "likes."

More investigations aimed directly at understanding self-concept translation as it occurs in school settings are needed. Success in differentiating courses of progress through the three translation processes and determining whether a typical sequence exists should permit the formulation of hypotheses about earlier translation behavior and perhaps even about self-concept formation. As data derived from the testing of such hypotheses accumulate, it will become possible to plan viable strategies for facilitating optimal self-concept development.

Exploratory Behavior

A central activity in the formation and clarification of self concepts is exploration. The individual explores his own attributes and the environment in which he finds himself. The processes of translation described above occur largely through exploratory behavior. The extent to which effective translation of self concepts results from school activities is likely to be a function of the extent to which those activities are truly exploratory.

Exploration in vocational development is not well understood. Jordaan (1963) proposed a schematic representation of self structure as a framework for considering exploratory behavior as it relates to occupational self concepts. But exploratory behavior is complex and difficult to study. Events sometimes serve exploratory purposes even when they are not intended to. A particular event can be useful as exploration from the behaver's internal point of view but not be evident as such externally. The opposite incongruity is also possible. It is likely that very important exploratory opportunities are missed because the individual or an important figure in his environment (possibly a counselor or teacher) is not tuned in to the prospects. Probably many experiences are simply "passed through" with minimal impact when only a little attention to exploration (looking for meaning, testing limits, relating to other experience, trying a different way) may have resulted in meaningful clarification of self-perceptions.

Jordaan's work has generated some study (O'Hara, 1969), but it is just beginning. Major advances in theory could accrue as a result of improved understanding of exploratory behavior, so it is important that it be studied. Jordaan's essay is an excellent point from which to begin.

Self-Concept Development

If the relationship between translation of self concepts and employment is not fully understood, it can be seen that the one between self-concept formation and employment is even less so. Since differences in readiness to cope with vocational developmental tasks appear before adolescence, it is important to try to address those differences early in order to move in the direction of equalized opportunities for development.

With the self report as the major vehicle for data collection, problems are encountered in learning about the self concepts of younger children. Limited vocabulary, lack of sophistication about language structure, and incomplete development of conceptual abilities probably combine to impede management of the cognitive demands in reporting about self concepts. Therefore, it seems reasonable to consider the affective components of self concepts. It seems reasonable as well to expect that even though young people may have difficulty reporting ideas about themselves, they will manage to express their feelings. Statements about the feeling tone of self concepts are often expressed in terms of self-esteem.

Self-Esteem

Self-esteem is one of the metadimensions identified by Super. Other investigators, though not using the term metadimension, have proposed a conceptualization which appears similar. As metadimensions are intended to assess commonalities across traits of self concepts, so other formulations have used self-esteem as a dimension of other dimensions. The work of Fitts (1972a,b,c) and his associates, for example, has produced three internal dimensions and five external dimensions of self concepts, arranged for scoring purposes as a three-by-five matrix. It is possible to compute a self-esteem score for each of the other categories, whatever their content. Other scores are computed across the basic dimensions, too, but self-esteem is the one of interest in the present context. Coopersmith's (1959) use of self-esteem appears different at first glance, but can be construed as similar to metadimensions on closer examination. What he calls "types of self-esteem" can be seen as evaluative ratings of self in several roles, such as school and family. Korman's (1966) definition of self-esteem as the subject's general evaluation of himself is not unrelated. Presumably general evaluation reflects many roles and various attributes implemented in those roles.

Self-Esteem and Behavior in School

Thompson (1972) reported that young people tend to have low self-esteem. While several dimensions of self concepts tended to increase with age, that was not necessarily the case with self-esteem. In an extensive cross-sectional study of boys (alternate years, grades two through twelve), Shultz (1965) found that while scores on other metadimensions (clarity and regnancy) increased, self-esteem decreased over the school years. The tendency for self-esteem scores to remain constant or perhaps decrease while other self concept scores increase suggests a caution. Why should self-esteem behave differently? If crystallization for disliked occupations and translation of self concepts into nonpreferred occupational terms both precede their positive counterparts, it may be that negative self-perceptions are clarified before positive ones. It is reasonable conjecture that reported measures of self-esteem might be affected by such a tendency. It should be possible to formulate and test hypotheses about the differential clarity of positive and negative statements about self.

Thompson (1972) reported that black students in junior and senior high school have lower self-esteem than whites. McGee (1971) made the same observation about fifth-grade boys. Both of them found positive relationships between self-esteem and academic variables: McGee with intelligence, and general achievement; Thompson with verbal ability and language development; both with reading level. Because nonwhites are disproportionately represented among low income groups, ethnic and socioeconomic influences can get confused. Careful study is needed to sort them out. Socioeconomic differences probably account for this observed difference in large measure. Inasmuch as the academic variables represent potential success in school, it can be hypothesized that related differences in self-esteem will increase over time. Consequently, self-esteem will be related to rate of progress through vocational developmental tasks. Unless change in the trend can be effected, those who are low in self-esteem in the middle grades will probably be less ready than their classmates to face the demands of work when the time comes.

Self-Esteem and Employment

Bailey (1970) found self-esteem to be related to self-concept growth and elaboration. On the basis of that finding, one could hypothesize that people high in self-esteem are likely to manifest more effective translation of self concepts into occupational terms than those low in self-esteem. Fitts (1972b) reported a comparison of women who did and did not drop out of training programs. The drop outs were lower in self-esteem. He also reported an inverse relationship between self-esteem and need for training in interpersonal skills. He found employed mothers to be higher in self-esteem than unemployed mothers. Korman (1967b, 1969) found self-esteem related to vocational behavior in students and workers and related to satisfaction (1967a).

On the basis of limited data and intuition, self-esteem seems related to a number of dimensions of work and work-related experience. It would be useful to study self-esteem as it relates to those experiences. Study in the context of early work experience, such as in part-time jobs while subjects are still in school, would offer several advantages. If counseling could be available to workers in relation to adjustment difficulties, counselors would be able to gain clinical impressions of how workers perceived themselves and translated those perceptions. Those impressions could be used to generate hypotheses. Close examination of modification of self concepts as a result of experience would also be possible. Under circumstances of relatively little commitment to a job, it may be possible for workers to examine themselves in relation to job requirements in fairly objective ways, more so than if they were in a full-time job seen as necessary to meet family obligations. The relationship between self-esteem and satisfaction may be particularly suitable for investigation under these circumstances.

Self-Esteem and Exploration

From earlier discussion of exploratory behavior, it is clear that people who are open to new experience will benefit more (or at least more efficiently) from exploration. Thompson (1972) reported findings that seem to bear on this relationship. People who are below average in self-esteem tend to be above average in defensiveness. They would probably resist certain kinds of feedback related to new experience. He also found low-esteem people unable to engage in self-disclosure at levels high enough to benefit from counseling. Presumably, then, their ability to take advantage of other opportunities for exploration of self would also be limited.

Fitts (1972b) found people with low self-esteem maintaining greater distance between self and others and between self and environment than people with high self-esteem. Vacchiano and others (1968) found that people who score low on self-esteem measures tend to be unwilling to try new experiences. Both of these reports permit inferences that low-esteem people are limited in ability to profit from exploration.

If people who are low in self-esteem are less able to profit from exploratory experience than their high self-esteem peers, then they are at a disadvantage in meeting developmental tasks. Because of that unreadiness, they will meet successive tasks with less and less adequacy; they will fall further and further behind in development.

Demonstrating that the inferred relationship between self-esteem and exploration does indeed exist would not establish cause and effect. It seems reasonable to hypothesize, however, that self-esteem needs to be adequate before exploration can be expected to be profitable. If so, then it is incumbent upon school people to *provide ample opportunities to increase self-esteem* if they intend to facilitate exploration.

There is some theoretical justification for the hypothesis stated in the preceding paragraph. Maslow (1954) proposed a hierarchical arrangement of human needs in which the lower order needs are prepotent to the higher order needs. That is, lower order needs must be relatively satisfied before higher order needs can become consistent motivants of behavior. Only part of that hierarchy is relevant to the present discussion, so the rest of it will not be considered.

The need for achievement falls fairly high in the hierarchy, and achievement is the principal business of schools. The need for self-esteem is prepotent to the need for achievement, so self-esteem must be established substantially before the need for achievement can become a consistent motivant. Maslow did not discuss exploration, but it can be seen as one instrument of achievement. On the basis of this formulation, if schools are to achieve their primary mission, self-esteem must be provided for. Those students who are high in self-esteem are better equipped to achieve, to receive the rewards that schools offer.

What about self-esteem, how can it be enhanced? Prepotent to the need for self-esteem is the need for love, belonging, and acceptance. Assuring adequate levels of self-esteem in students may require meeting the need for acceptance and love.

Maslow's definition of self-esteem is not precisely identical to the others used here. The formulation seems usable nonetheless. The relationships between acceptance and self-esteem and and between self-esteem and achievement make sense. The exact point where exploration may fit into those relationships is uncertain. An attractive hypothesis about the place of exploration is that a major function of exploratory behavior is learning how to esteem oneself and what to esteem in oneself. On the basis of earlier discussion, perhaps an important step in learning to esteem oneself is to identify those things not esteemed, to clarify negative self-perceptions. Perhaps the process requires "elimination" of negative attributes from consideration before positive ones can be sifted in useful ways.

Behavioral scientists can study the relationship between self-esteem and exploration, and in due course, the process will be better understood. School personnel cannot wait "until all the data are' in" before deciding how they will intervene in that process. Those who choose to act in ways intended to enhance self-esteem and facilitate exploration can expect very little help in the form of data, some theoretical support, and a great deal of personal opinion. The best course to follow is to form an alliance of practitioner and researcher working together to accomplish precision of formulation and quick conversion of findings into practice.

Summary

This chapter reviewed some of the theory about occupational self concepts and some of the data about their measurement. Particular attention was given to the translation of self concepts into occupational terms and to exploratory behavior. Self-esteem, as a variable in vocational behavior, was considered, especially in its relationship to exploration. Some investigational and operational problems were identified, and some hypotheses relevant to the modification of theory and practice were proposed.

4

Facilitating Career Development in Schools

On the basis of the data analysis and discussion presented in the previous two chapters it can be seen that the facilitation of career development in schools is a complex process. Many school programs seem to be based on the assumption that all young people are at the same level of readiness to make the vocationally relevant decisions expected of them. Since they are not, some kind of change is in order. Practitioners, of course, readily acknowledge that important differences exist among individuals and groups. However, program offerings often do not provide adequately for such differences. Although there is some evidence of change, as in improved educational offerings for those not planning to attend college, much remains to be done.

Doing what remains to be done and effecting program change are difficult to accomplish. That fact combined with excessive demands on professional time and insufficient resources may lead some to stop trying. The enhancement of opportunities for career development does sometimes seem to be a hopelessly difficult task. Without concerted effort, though, substantial portions of the student body will continue to be neglected, to be deprived of opportunities that ought to be theirs. The launching of concerted effort which can attain the implied goals requires at least two basic tools: (1) a theoretical framework within which to make decisions about building programs and offering experiences; and (2) knowledge of what other practitioners have tried. Available theory is not complete, by any means, but it is the theory we have, and it must be used. It can be improved only through application and the modification of ideas that results from systematic analysis of them in practice.

This chapter will examine some practices that have been employed or proposed in relation to preparing youth for employment. Most attention will be directed to guidance programs and practices, but an occasional excursion outside the operating realm of counselors may occur. A central thesis will be that theory and practice are essentially inseparable even though there are times when they must be considered apart from each other. The most practical tool a worker has is a sound theoretical framework; the ultimate support for a theoretical idea is effective application. They must supplement each other, and modify each other, in order to grow. The suggestions offered in this chapter rest on the assumption that practitioner and theorist can work together for the improvement of services.

The chapter will begin with a discussion of guidance staff needs and counselors' related options. Brief consideration will be directed to information services in guidance. Vocational behavior will be discussed in terms of vocational maturity, self-perceptions, special groups of students. The chapter will end with a discussion of exploration.

The Guidance Staff

Service to students is the most important consideration in guidance programs, and they should be organized to serve that purpose (Humes, 1971). As seen above, however, the services that guidance programs are expected to provide have grown enormously. A design for counseling services that has been less than adequate in the past is being charged with the responsibility of increasingly complex effort (McNeil, 1965). Some counselors report that even though they are interested in providing career guidance, they are hard pressed to find the time to do so. Increased service is possible only through increasing resources, increasing productivity with present resources, or narrowing the scope of service.

Increasing Guidance Resources

The National Advisory Council on Vocational Education (NACVE, 1972) has called for increased appropriations at the federal level to support guidance services. That same report indicates that the student-to-counselor ratio was cut in half between 1958 and 1968, but has declined little since the latter date. At a time when the trend appears to be to level off on staff development and budget makers are actively trying to reduce expenditures, it is not easy to be optimistic that resources will increase.

Counselors, and other related staff, should continue to work to elevate their service to a central role in the school organization (Haettenschwiller and Jabs, 1969). Success at that effort will certainly help to maintain present resources. Whether it helps to increase them depends on the effectiveness of service. Such effectiveness is difficult to demonstrate in any case, but particularly so when resources are not adequate. Counselors should also strive for working conditions that permit them to demonstrate their effectiveness.

Increasing the Productivity of Guidance Staff

A variety of suggestions as to how guidance workers can improve productivity have appeared in the literature. Some have suggested the use of teaching staff to serve some purposes in this connection. It is probably true that the presence of guidance counselors has led teachers to make referrals where, in the absence of such specialists, they would have done what they could on their own. However, teachers may resent having the referrals simply returned to them on the grounds that "it is their responsibility" to take care of the situation. Counselors have to respond positively to such referrals. One way to respond is to help teachers cope with the problems they encounter. If teachers are going to be helpful in achieving some of the purposes of guidance programs, then they probably have to learn that it is in their own best interest to do so. Lewellyn and Grace (1960) proposed a six-step process in which academic staff were used as advisors to help students examine their own values and implementation of them. How such faculty members acquired the appropriate skills was not indicated, but presumably counselors served as trainers. Where counselors have the necessary skills to do that kind of training, it is desirable to do so. To the fullest extent possible, guidance purposes ought to be served in the classroom. Accomplishing that requires high levels of cooperation between teachers and counselors. Consulting with teachers may be a way to achieve cooperation, and it will have a reciprocal effect when it is well done. As consulting is successful, and teachers feel competent and supported, cooperative efforts will multiply. Anandam and Williams (1971) reported that assisting teachers in this fashion helps them to feel more positive toward the children with whom they work. Counselors who effectively promote that kind of response from teachers can reach a larger number of students than they can on their own resources. Procedures which accomplish that end are to be encouraged. In the long run, if not immediately, counselors should find more time to spend on services they feel they have neglected. Presumably that means more time to be given to vocational concerns.

NACVE Recommendations

The National Advisory Council on Vocational Education (NACVE, 1972) stated three recommendations related to uses of staff time and skills. That report suggested that counselors need improved skills in career guidance, that the ratio of students to counselors be reduced so effective service can be afforded all students, and that provision be made for wide use of paraprofessionals working under the supervision of qualified counselors. Each of those suggestions warrants passing attention here.

Career Guidance Skills

An important emphasis (as implied in the NACVE statement) in improving counselors' career guidance skills must be in-service training. Expansion of guidance programs appears to have leveled off, so the opportunities to effect change simply through the addition of new staff are substantially less than they were a decade ago. The tendency for guidance to focus on a wide range of concerns other than career development has left many practitioners with limited skills in the area either because the skills were never achieved or they have fallen into disuse.

There is an additional reason why in-service rather than pre-service education is indicated in improving career guidance skills. Where counselors are not actively engaged in career guidance activities, it is likely that the program they work in has a different, broader focus. Therefore, it may be necessary not only to improve their personal skills but to equip them with skills to execute strategies that lead to change. This purpose seems to be served effectively when specific situational considerations are dealt with.

Student-Counselor Ratio

This is not the place to examine student-counselor ratio in detail, but one important observation can be made. From Conant's (1959) early recommendation to the present time there seems to be an assumption that a universal ratio is appropriate, that all programs and all schools can function effectively on the same ratio. It makes more sense to this writer to consider student-counselor ratio as a function of the purposes of the guidance program. Thus, some purposes might be served by a relatively high ratio of students per counselor, but others might require a very low ratio.

Paraprofessional Staff

The use of paraprofessionals in guidance programs warrants careful study. Just what jobs can be done by such staff and which tasks qualified counselors are willing to relinquish are considerations that need attention. The prospect of gaining support for the use of paraprofessionals, however, seems in doubt. There was no landswell of acceptance of paraprofessionals in the early and mid-1960s when there were serious personnel shortages. Present surpluses of professionally trained workers seem likely to reduce rather than increase the acceptance of paraprofessionals.

Although immediate acceptance seems unlikely, effort needs to be directed to the study of contributions paraprofessionals can make. Some (Schlossberg, 1967) have seen them as improving services; others (Patterson, 1965) have advised caution. The important consideration is really the effect of their presence on clients. It is possible to gain the impression that sometimes the central consideration has been the counselor's convenience rather than the client's welfare.

Narrowing the Scope of Guidance Services

If the observations made in Chapter 1 are accurate, then the prospect of narrowing the scope of guidance services will be unpopular with many counselors. Even though counselors are inclined to try to do too many things, they will not necessarily welcome efforts to reduce demands on their time. They see themselves as helpers, and they seek every opportunity to implement that self-perception. Modification in that tendency, to be effective, will have to come from counselors themselves.

Two conditions seem to be prerequisite to counselors' taking initiative in the modification of their helping style. First, they will have to accept a redefinition of help. One aspect of that redefinition involves a question of what actually constitutes help for various types of students; another involves the relative effectiveness of various forms of delivering service: individual counseling, group counseling and other group activities, or environmental intervention. Both of these aspects of the helping relationship need careful study by practitioners and researchers to help counselors decide on the most efficient ways to use their time.

The other condition to be met is that counselors must learn how to decide which requests for help to decline. This involves accepting the fact that they cannot help everyone. Sometimes it is not possible to be helpful because of limited personal or physical resources, sometimes because of the state of the science, and sometimes because help is not wanted. Accepting the possibility of spending less time in impossible tasks is an important way to narrow the scope of what is attempted. Acting on that acceptance requires courage.

Another way to narrow the scope is to concentrate on offering the kind of help that clients really want. Evidence is clear that students in school expect help from counselors with career planning. Whether they really expect help in other behavioral areas is less clear. Concentration on the area where help is wanted would permit further narrowing of the scope of endeavor. This is not to say that personal problems should be avoided. It is only to suggest that the expected help—that dealing with vocational problems—be given priority.

Setting of priorities is to be encouraged in other activities as well. Examination of effectiveness should receive high priority in time usage with a view to improving service. The position that one is too busy to find out whether his time is well spent is hard to defend. In the final analysis, the effectiveness of guidance services will be a function of the time and effort spent in improving them.

It may be within the power of counselors to improve guidance services by means of any of the processes described in this section. Whatever happens, much of the initiative will have to come from counselors in defining their own identity, obtaining resources, or modifying program goals. Counselor education both for candidates in training and for practitioners on the job must be designed to help them with those tasks. But the decision as to which course to follow lies with the counselors.

Information Services

The unquestionable importance of information to vocational maturity underscores the need for counselors to offer functional information services to students. In this area, perhaps more than any other, departure from traditional methods is in order. It is not profitable for counselors to spend time on tasks that computers can do so much more efficiently. It is almost a certainty that before long counselors will be relieved of most information storage and retrieval tasks respecting national labor force data, occupational requirements, and educational opportunities. Freedom from those tasks will permit attention to others where human participation is needed.

The future of local information about employment and educational opportunities is less certain. Eventually, local data are likely to be stored for electronic retrieval, but in the meantime (and even after such storage is effected), counselors may be able to help teachers accomplish some of the informational objectives of guidance programs through suitable efforts. The Central Jersey Industry-Education Council has found some success in helping teachers to plan for visits by community speakers and to conduct field trips (Novick, 1968 and 1969). These efforts not only accomplish important guidance objectives (delivering occupational information to students) but they are seen by teachers as helpful to them. Teachers who are pleased with what happens in guidance programs can do much to foster the success of those programs.

Another quite different suggestion about the use of information is indicated. The manner in which a counselor conceptualizes the classification of occupations can affect the way he relates to changes of preference expressed by students. The way in which counselors and students alike conceive the relatedness of occupations can influence the way they plan together for exploratory experiences. All systems for the classification of occupations have some weaknesses that bear on understanding similarities and differences among occupations and avenues of movement from one to another (Super, 1957). Empirical studies have recently lent support to one formulation that can be useful to counselors in the connection just discussed. Roe and her co-workers (1966) found support for the idea that occupational groups are, in fact, related as she conceptualized them. That is, they found that when people change jobs, they are most likely to move to another job within the same field. If they change to a different field, it is likely to be one adjacent to the field they leave rather than a distant one. Counselors are in a position to record data as to whether students follow a similar pattern when they talk about preferences. They might also keep records of students' reactions to part-time jobs and other exploratory activities to determine differences in the use of those experiences when work and identified vocational interest are in the same or different fields. Practicing counselors can formulate other hypotheses about this relationship that can be investigated on the job without extensive resources.

Facilitating Vocational Maturity

As evidence accumulates about the nature of vocational maturity, the complexity of the construct is evidenced. An early study (Super and Overstreet, 1960) found five factors of vocational maturity in ninth-grade boys. Analysis of some of the same data plus other data collected later in the lives of the same subjects (Jordaan, 1972) yielded

19 factors. On the basis of work done with the Attitude Scale of his Vocational Development Inventory, Crites (1969) has formulated four group factors of vocational maturity. It is necessary to underscore the multidimensional character of vocational maturity to make it clear that the following discussion touches on only a limited number of the variables which contribute to it. Some attitudinal and some cognitive components of vocational maturity are treated in the following paragraphs.

Attitudinal Components of Vocational Maturity

The principal investigations of vocational attitudes and their relationship to vocational maturity have been reported by Crites (1969). Interpretation of the results of several studies led him to postulate a general developmental dimension, adjustment, which is related to both the maturity of vocational attitudes and educational achievement. Better adjusted adolescents are seen by their teachers and counselors as advanced educationally and mature vocationally. Experience which contributes to the general adjustment of adolescents also contributes to their vocational maturity.

Other findings reported by Crites are of interest to practicing counselors. Maturity of vocational attitudes was found to be related to persistence in college, success in some vocational training curricula, and job success. These findings suggest that replication of the same studies be undertaken and related hypotheses formulated and tested.

Crites reported mixed findings respecting the relationship between counseling and maturity of vocational attitudes. Some findings indicated that counseling has a positive influence on vocational attitudes; others did not. Studies of this relationship, where the quality of counseling can be assured, if they produce positive results, could be an important step toward demonstrating that vocational counseling is effective. Operating counselors can contribute to this effort by testing hypotheses about the relationship between vocational attitudes and differing kinds of counselor contact with students, such as individual counseling or group counseling. The effect of various noncounseling activities on students might also be tested.

Cognitive Components of Vocational Maturity

In an early effort to help eighth-grade students make wiser choices and decisions, Gribbons (1960) interviewed 108 students before and after group counseling. He concluded that postponement of choice of high school curriculum to the end of ninth grade would result in fewer errors. He also concluded that the experience accelerated vocational development. Since postponement of decisions is an unlikely prospect, the latter conclusion will be considered here in relation to some cognitive variables in vocational maturity.

Decision-Making Behavior

Evans and Cody (1969) studied the relative effects of directed and nondirected practice in acquisition and transfer of decision-making skills in 60 eighth graders. They found directed practice to be more effective in both cases. They also found no sex differences. Data of this kind indicate not only that decision making can be taught, but that some methods of learning it may be superior to others. The extent to which students can learn relevant decision-making behavior at earlier ages is unknown. How it happens that some students acquire different decision-making skills is also unknown. Counselors can help to initiate programs to study the acquisition of decision-making skills in school settings. Perhaps they can also influence decisions about specific content where decision making is already being taught. They might suggest that vocational decisions be the content and help to study outcomes so instruction can be modified on the basis of data. They might advance the Lewellyn and Grace (1960) observation that the process should move from the student's present position toward consideration of the vocational objective, rather than in the opposite direction. It may even be possible for them to give serious consideration to the proposal (Davies, 1971) that decision making be the only vocational behavior addressed in schools, that others be abandoned.

Some students who need particular assistance with decision-making skills are those who, for a variety of reasons, lack confidence in their own knowledge as a basis for making decisions. Vassos (1971) found peer influence effective in helping students to understand the importance of their own knowledge. Careful analysis of the decision-making behavior of students can permit counselors to identify specific components of the process with which some students encounter difficulty. The use of peers as assistants in coping with identified difficulties may prove effective in some of those areas.

Planning Behavior

The description of readiness to learn vocational planning offered in Chapter 2 is based on logical extensions of knowledge rather than on data. Some provocative possibilities for study are implied in that formulation. Accepting the assumption that planning skills can be taught, one can proceed to study at what age levels and under what circumstances young people can learn planning in schools.

That mastery of planfulness differs among adolescents has been well demonstrated in the Career Pattern Study. Gribbons and Lohnes (1965) concluded that vocational maturity of junior high school students may be underestimated. They found evidence of educational and vocational planfulness in their subjects. Relating that conclusion to one that Gribbons (1960) reached lends some support to the idea of trying to teach planfulness. The exact form that such instruction should take remains to be determined. One suggestion that seems relevant, although it did not arise in relation to planning, was offered by Mayer and Carlson (1971). They proposed the use of a technique they called fading, that is, the gradual reduction of guidelines. In approaching instruction in planfulness, highly structured guidelines might be employed in the beginning and gradually reduced as students acquired some skill. Counselors can be instrumental in gaining knowledge about the effectiveness of such procedures.

As in other studies, Vriend (1969) found planning accounting for a major share of vocational maturity ratings. He concluded that the incorporation of vocationally relevant material in the total educational experience of twelfth graders can modify and influence the course of vocational development in both sexes in all curricula. Of particular interest in the present context is his observation that such intervention has an impact on the sense of fatalism that many young people have about the future. If they can learn to believe that some control of their destiny lies in their own hands, they can learn to plan. If that outcome was observed at the twelfth-grade level, perhaps it can occur earlier. Specific attention to the emergence of planning skills through the school years can help to identify just how those skills are acquired. Such knowledge can be put to use in attempting to accelerate vocational developmental processes.

Predicting Vocational Behavior

It is appropriate to consider prediction of vocational behavior in close proximity to planning. When young people master vocational planfulness, they have, in a sense, managed accurate prediction of their own behavior. As efforts are undertaken to teach students to plan, an early focus in that process can profitably be prediction of their own performance. Fretz (1972) recommended increased attention to prediction of career preference even in preadolescence, but MacArthur and Mosychuk (1966) found that less effective at grades six and seven for lower socioeconomic groups than for others. To be effective in helping others to predict, counselors need to sharpen their own skills at prediction. In making predictions, counselors are accustomed to relying heavily on test scores. In helping others to predict accurately, other kinds of data should be put to use as well.

Many students report that they think counselors do not know them well. At least part of the time, it is clear that those students do not regard test data as the crucial elements in knowing them. Students often object to being characterized by the probability statements that test data represent. Counselors can help them to understand such statements in the context of other information that keeps them in touch with their own uniqueness. They can help students to use other kinds of information to predict their own behavior and to modify the prob- ability statements that can be made from tests.

Possible approaches to instruction in self-prediction can be seen in Brenner's (1968) study of the relationship between high school data and job performance. His finding that teachers make meaningful discriminations of work habits could be of use to students, particularly if teachers' observations are reported in supportive ways and in terms that are seen as relevant to performance in work settings. The same use of information on attendance is possible. Even minimal success on the part of students in predicting their own work habits and attendance over the short run is likely to have an important effect on both.

Assistance in short-range prediction of one's own behavior makes sense especially for students who face particular difficulty in meeting their educational or vocational objectives. Newman (1966), through interviewing 34 vocational school dropouts, determined that adverse school experience, financial need, and negative parental attitudes toward education were offered frequently as reasons for lack of school success. Counselors and students could work together in anticipating adverse experiences in school and planning alternative ways of responding to them. In effect, students could predict the outcomes of their own behavior. Counselors might also work with teachers to minimize the frustrations that students experience with curriculum and subject matter.

Coping with financial need problems may be more difficult. It may help counselors to be aware that financial need is reported more frequently by boys (Adams, 1964) than girls as a school-related problem, and of Newman's 34 subjects, 27 were boys. Assistance with finding part-time jobs is an obvious possibility, but the students of concern here may be the ones who have difficulty with employers under ordinary circumstances. Special arrangements with employers are also possible but difficult to secure. Some employers are willing to help, though, so counselors and other school personnel should persist in trying to work out suitable plans. On occasion, students work out individual arrangements with employers whom they locate through their own resources. Alert counselors will help them to use such opportunities to advantage. Since monetary incentive (Pope, 1966) has been shown to work, all possible forms of reimbursement for accomplishment should be explored.

Seim (1970) reported success in getting parents to visit school in relation to their children's progress through evening counseling sessions. One reason for their reluctance to visit the school was that they felt they could not dress well enough for affairs like PTA meetings.

Using test data in atypical ways offers some possibilities for helping students to predict their own short-run behavior. It has become common to have students predict their performance on interest inventories and then deal with the discrepancies between predicted and obtained scores. Students can project varying images in test response (McCall, 1965) as well. On some tests, students can be asked to respond as the kind of person an employer would hire. Discrepancies between these and actual scores can be the basis for planning change of behavior in directions chosen by the student. Data such as Hewer's (1965) that students tend to prefer occupations in the same interest field as their fathers, might be used in a related way. A student could select a preferred occupation in an interest area quite different from his father's and "guess" the test responses that produce a desirable profile. Again discrepancies between these and actual scores would serve as a basis for planning strategies to change in a desired direction. Success with managing change under supervision ought to help students to move toward directing change in their own lives with their own resources (see Kratochvil and others, 1970).

Undoubtedly, counselors can identify other ideas for stimulating student interest in prediction. There are two important points to remember. One is to learn enough about the processes required for success in these activities so that practitioners can become competent in evoking and maintaining student involvement in the prediction of their own behavior and the planning of their own destiny. The other is that students decide the direction of change they want to try to effect.

Acquisition of Work-Related Skills in School

Many adolescents manage to accumulate through the course of their development adequate skills to qualify for jobs or related education. By and large, it is the academic achievers, the vocationally mature, who do so. Even if they do not learn specific job skills, their general skills serve them in meeting some occupational or educational demands and their general achievements permit rapid mastery of others. Vocationally immature adolescents, often nonachievers, are less successful and need particular help in preparing to meet work-related expectations.

Experience in working with nonachieving adolescents seeking employment indicates that they are simply overwhelmed by the expectations they encounter in personnel and employment offices. They often seem quite unprepared to cope with interviews and even application forms. In anticipation of such difficulties, counselors sometimes try to give school dropouts some last-minute instructions, either written or oral, about what to expect and how to respond. Many more carefully planned efforts occur as well, but students sometimes report that credibility is lacking. Students may find efforts to help with job-seeking skills unbelievable for many reasons, not just because they are not well conceived or well executed. In fact, the best efforts may be ineffective because of student attitudes and expectations. When the aim is to reach students who are probably disaffected with school, it is probably desirable to create an appearance of being as unlike school as possible.

Neel (1971) reported conducting a workshop for students on job seeking. The workshop idea is certainly different from the usual school activity and, therefore, appealing to some students. Requiring application and registration in order to participate may widen the appeal. Conducting the workshop off school grounds is certain to appeal to some. Having the same workshop open to registrants from several school districts at the same time would create the aura of a convention and permit some students to feel they were being treated as adults. The last arrangement would permit several school staffs to work cooperatively capitalizing on particular talents and exposing students to authorities not associated with their own school problems. Each dimension of differentness can increase the appeal of this kind of experience for some students. For some, taking part in the planning would be especially appealing. It might increase the relevance of content as well.

Over the long run, it is to be expected that continuous experience will be more productive than last-minute instruction, no matter how dramatic the latter is. During the course of the school life of a student, many tasks of various kinds are assigned to students. Sometimes the resulting experience may have developmental importance. At least some such "slots" at some levels could be filled as if they were job openings (see Leonard and others, 1968). Vacancies could be advertised, applications filed, interviews conducted, and selections made. Performance reports could be recorded, and students could learn to prepare a resume of work experiences. Probably some incentive system could be devised. Procedures would have to become more complex and more similar to actual work settings through the grades.

Several steps in the process could generate profitable learning experiences. The interview, in particular, could be designed to facilitate exploration. Caution would have to be exercised to assure that nonachieving students had adequate opportunities to achieve success. The fundamental purpose would be defeated if this kind of structure became another case of providing the most help for those who need it the least.

At first glance, the implementation of such a plan appears to pose enormous scheduling problems. Gaining acceptance of the general purposes is an important first step. Beginning on a limited basis and providing for gradual expansion is recommended. Close cooperation among teachers and counselors would facilitate incorporation of the entire scheme into the school's routine.

A suggestion can be taken from Witczak and Ehlers (1970) to reinforce any positive outcomes of the kind of project just described. They recommended congratulatory letters be sent in recognition of particular achievements related to occupational tasks. It is a common practice to reward academic achievement in this fashion A comparable but legitimate system of rewards for nonachievers might serve to restore confidence in education on the part of some students who do not ordinarily receive the academic accolades.

Some more comprehensive efforts to incorporate preparation for work into the mainstream of education have been tried. Weil (1970) studied one such program which was designed expressly for school dropouts. At the Education Center for Youth in Newark, New Jersey, a program was established to facilitate self-discovery for both personal and community advantage. Enrollees (maintained at 100) alternated between one week at school and one at work. Thus, each of 50 positions, distributed among seven cooperating employers, was filled by two enrollees. Typically enrollees were nonwhite, from lower-income families, and represented a broad range of academic ability.

Weil studied 288 enrollees who had either dropped out (98) or graduated (190) between December 1964 and August 1969. He found the "holding power" of the Education Center for Youth to be 66.0 percent compared to 30.5 percent for an evening adult high school in Newark. Comparison with the adult school may not be meaningful, but the 66 percent graduation rate among enrollees, all of whom had once been school dropouts, is of significance. Three of the factors positively related to holding power (time out of school, age on entering the Center, and grade at time of leaving regular high school) are probably related to vocational maturity. Thus, even among these relatively immature enrollees, it seems possible to differentiate levels of vocational maturity. The other related variable was occupation while at the Center. The lowest graduation rate (43.2 percent) was found among those who worked as service station attendants. Rewards for educational attainment were more visible at other job sites.

Floundering was common among enrollees before they entered the Center. For many, it continued after beginning the program, but it proceeded under supervision, so to speak. Counseling was available to enrollees, and supervisors on the job cooperated in finding compatible circumstances of employment for each enrollee. Apparently these opportunities to have adult and expert assistance with specific developmental tasks contributed to success. Through imaginative extension of the practices reported by Weil, it may be possible to facilitate similar progress in adolescents before they drop out of school in the first place.

Groups with Special Needs

Vocational counselors accept responsibility to work with people in any context related to vocational behavior. Much knowledge about career development applies to all people, but there are some groups who are of particular concern because their access to developmental and employment opportunities is often restricted. Counselors need to be aware of how general theory and practice are and are not applicable to special groups. Three groups of special concern will be discussed in this section: women, the culturally different, and the disabled.

Women

That women experience different developmental opportunities from men cannot be disputed. The effect of that difference is probably as dramatic in occupational expectations and opportunities as in any other realm of behavior. Differences between women and men are great enough that Tiedeman and O'Hara (1963) suggested a separate theory may be required to describe the career behavior of women. Rose and Elton (1971) recommended specifically that personality determinants of occupational choice need to be regarded separately for the sexes. Discontinuity has been noted in the careers of women (Miller and Form, 1951) and particularly in the decisiveness of vocational behavior during the eleventh grade (Hollender, 1971). Women have been differentiated as "career" and "noncareer" oriented (Astin, 1968).

Regarding women at work or seeking work reveals other differences from men. In an analysis of data available on work applications at a state employment service office, Hume (1967) found that 47 percent of the women and 19 percent of the men seeking employment were high school graduates, and that 90 percent of the women and 21 percent of the men reported no work-related interests. Apparently, even though female job applicants are better educated than males, they have fewer crystallized vocational preferences. This could be a result of a "non-career" orientation, but such a high proportion is unlikely. It is probably the result of differential developmental experience. Reinforcement of such difference may continue beyond school. In a recent study of Neighborhood Youth Corps enrollees (Freeberg, 1968), both counselors and work supervisors evaluated males on the basis of intellectual capabilities and females on the basis of attitudinal conformity.

In attempting to offer special service to girls and women, counselors are handicapped because of gaps in research about the development of girls (Lewis, 1965). Even though their vocational adjustment and occupational progress have received increasing attention in recent years and some advances have occurred, the gaps remain. Counseling has been shown to be effective in helping intellectually superior women to break through restrictive social practices toward greater self-actualization (Drews, 1965). If further progress is to occur, it is necessary to stress family roles for boys and occupational roles for girls during development and to stop encouraging girls toward limited occupational goals under the pretext of being realistic (Rossi, 1965). Counselors have an obligation to help girls confront their internal occupational stereotypes and to plan strategies for coping with restrictive practices.

The Culturally Different

Young people whose development occurs outside the mainstream of American middle-class culture often experience educational and other socioeconomic restrictions Behavioral scientists have not reached consensus on causes and effects of observed characteristics in the culturally different, but disproportionate numbers of some groups (notably blacks, Spanish-speaking people, and American Indians) are represented among the poor. The combined impact of low income and exclusionary practice results in socioeconomic disadvantage. Ultimately, that disadvantage has an effect on self-perception, a negative one, and that effect increases with age (Thompson, 1972).

Inability to sort out the differential influences of ethnic and socioeconomic factors on development has permitted confusion and controversy to prevail. Unwillingness to give up stereotypic characterizations which appear to serve some personal or economic advantage has tended to prolong both. Long-standing practices affected individual and group identity in ways that had come to be regarded by many as stable social patterns. Recent events have been marked by efforts to reshape those identities and restructure those social patterns. Such events also inevitably have an impact on self-perception.

The changing self-perceptions and the events that facilitated them have been productive for some, have stirred dreams and aspirations for many, and have compounded the confusion for others. All these reactions have vocational ramifications; all present special guidance requirements; all challenge the counselor's resources.

Vocational maturity among the culturally different lags behind the national average. Crites (1968) reported some ethnic differences, and others (e.g., Maynard and Hansen, 1970) have reported differences in inner-city youth, or between urban and suburban youth (Ansell and Hansen, 1971; Shappell and others, 1971).

The source of reported differences is not always identifiable. Maynard and Hansen found that differences among suburban youth and inner-city blacks and whites disappeared when intelligence was kept constant. Ansell and Hansen found that lower-class subjects were behind middle-class subjects in vocational development irrespective of race. They also reported large increases in vocational maturity scores in eleventh grade. Of course, that last observation reflects the fact that the least vocationally mature are the students who drop out of school before entering the eleventh grade.

Both Ansell and Hansen, and Shappell and his associates, concluded that socioeconomic status is more influential as a determinant of occupational orientation than sex is. That conclusion has to be considered in the light of Neale and Proshek's (1967) observation that sex role is less important in lower-class than in middle-class environments. Studies which control or partial out the effect of these two variables could clarify the nature of the relationship.

In the Shappell study reported above, it was found that inner-city youth are preoccupied with environmental concerns and suburban youth are primarily concerned with interpersonal goals. These investigators concluded that the concerns of inner-city youth need to be dispelled, or at least dealt with, in order to facilitate occupational development.

. All of the groups discussed in this section pose particular challenges to counselors. Siegel (1970) proposed that some can be reached by talking with them about their roles as members of the labor force. Since culturally different youth appear, in general, to be less ready than average to make the vocationally relevant decisions demanded in school (Ansell and Hansen, 1971), this may be a good beginning point. Shappell and his co-workers (1971) suggested that confidence-inspiring behavior on the part of the counselor can help to move students in the direction of vocational maturity. If counselors can be inspiring, that is to be welcomed. At least they can serve as good role models by performing well the decision-making and planning tasks of their own jobs and manifesting the satisfaction that they help others to seek. By these means they can have a positive impact on culturally different clients which could serve as the beginning of an important helping relationship.

The Disabled

People with a variety of disabilities face particular difficulties in coping with vocational expectations. Those who are mentally retarded, physically or neurologically impaired, chronically ill, emotionally disturbed, or have particular learning problems can press the counselor to the limits of his competency. Not only do they have difficulty in understanding their own potential or coping with the trauma of sudden change in self-perceptions, but they often encounter hesitant public acceptance.

Early work experience is almost always difficult either because the handicapped appear "different" and encounter suspicion or rejection, or because they do not appear different and their limitations are unnoticed or easily forgotten. Helping disabled adolescents to prepare for and succeed in early job experience is very demanding for most counselors. Finding developmental opportunities that help them is sometimes almost impossible precisely because of their disabilities. Often the parents of disabled youngsters also need assistance in understanding or accepting the vocational potential of their children.

Each of the special groups discussed, in its unique way, makes demands on the time and skills of counselors. Special needs are easy to overlook or avoid under the typical pressures of the working day. Counselors need the support of their administrators to find the resources needed to attend to the unique concerns of special groups. They also need help from behavioral scientists in understanding and finding solutions to perplexing developmental, placement, and adjustment problems.

Self Concepts

The discussion in Chapter 3 demonstrated the relationship between self concepts and some vocational behaviors. More generally, it has been observed that people with healthier self concepts tend to perform more satisfactorily than others (Fitts, 1972b). To facilitate satisfactory performance, both in general and vocationally, it is desirable that schools foster positive self-perception. Before discussing specifically what can be done in school settings to foster positive self-perceptions, some attention needs to be given to the relationship between self-perception and achievement, to self-esteem in general, and the relationship between self-esteem and employment.

Self-Perception and Achievement

Achievement has been found to be significantly related to self-perception on a number of dimensions. LeMay and Damm (1968) found 42 achievers to be more self actualizing than 42 underachievers in terms of directing their own lives, forming intimate relationships, applying their own values, sensitivity to their own needs, and self-acceptance of deficiencies and aggressive tendencies. The cause-and-effect relationship is not known from these data, but it is interesting to speculate about the possibilities that achievement would be improved by attention to self-actualizing behaviors and not just academic skills. Perhaps it would be possible to improve achievement (and consequently vocational maturity) through counseling specifically related to self-acceptance. Clinical experience tends to support such a hypothesis; school counselors can help to examine it systematically.

Some evidence has been offered by Gillham (1967) about the same relationship. She observed that an individual may be enslaved by preschool perceptions of being stupid or insignificant until some significant other helps him to learn otherwise. She reported several anecdotes of how reading teachers, aware of the importance of enhancing self concepts, departed from their instructional tasks to attend to feelings about self. Their efforts not only affected levels of self-esteem but improved academic performance as well.

According to Neale and Proshek (1967), schools are failing students by not teaching them to like academic experience. Their evidence indicates that young people tend to like themselves and school less as they grow older. Apparently, an important part of that perception (equivalent to a reduction in self-esteem) is the reinforcement received in schools in relation to achievement. Those who achieve well receive all of the rewards. Those who do not achieve well do not receive the rewards. Sometimes they are punished. Too often, they are made to feel that the lack of achievement is entirely their fault. At least part of the time, the school may be at fault for expecting too much or using ineffective instructional methods. The achievers feel good about themselves; the nonachievers feel bad.

Self-Esteem

At least two studies reported in Chapter 3 support the idea that the way people feel about themselves is related to the way they perform. The exact nature of that relationship is not well understood. It is certainly an oversimplification to say that the relationship is reciprocal, that positive feelings lead to good performance which reinforces positive feelings, and vice-versa. Such a statement leaves many events unexplained. Some observers have noted possible complications in that relationship.

Fitts (1972b) concluded that people who have less than optimal self concepts are likely to relate primarily to the noncognitive aspects of their own behavior. Freeberg (1968) found self-esteem to be strictly an attitudinal measure. In combination, these two ideas suggest the possibility that people who perceive themselves negatively are likely to respond to their own performance in terms of how they feel about it rather than in terms of an objective appraisal of its effectiveness. This tendency not only reinforces the negative self-esteem, but it presents obstacles to the introduction of concrete data about performance. Evidence that behavior is productive may not be readily incorporated into self-perceptions.

Havener and Izard (1962) studied seriously ill subjects, but their findings suggest possibilities for normal people as well. In the presence of unrealistic self-enhancement, they found tendencies toward overvaluation of self and undervaluation of others. They concluded that this combination results from failure to develop or maintain self-related positive affect. They speculated that the deficiency in self-related positive affect is a result of insufficient interpersonal rewards. Devaluation of others was seen as a defense against complete loss of self-related positive affect.

Under the conditions just described, it serves little purpose to point out to a student that he is really doing satisfactorily. If he is not ready to put that kind of information to use, an alternative course of action seems called for. An evident beginning point is to respond directly to the feeling/tone instead of attempting cognitive intervention, to provide some positive affect that he can perceive as self-related. Perceiving that he is esteemed by others facilitates enhancement of his self-esteem.

It is also necessary to provide opportunities in which the individual can achieve success. Initially, it is probably well to reward success but minimize assessment of it. As self-esteem increases evaluation of performance can be gradually introduced. Any experience that makes it possible for an individual to feel good about himself, to gain in self-esteem, increases his readiness to learn about himself and his environment. That kind of information is critical to the facilitation of self concept development. The more adequate information an individual has about himself and his environment, the more likely it is that he will find satisfying implementation of his occupational self concepts.

Exploration

The processes that lead ultimately to satisfying implementation of self concepts begin early in life and are influenced very much by school experience. In one view (Fitts, 1972b), the crucial period in the development of self concepts is the junior high school years. Junior high school is an important time particularly with respect to occupational self concepts. The individual is required to make decisions about his future, he is pressured to make an occupational commitment, his experiences may take on more specific vocational relevance than they did before, and exploration begins to intensify. The quality of exploratory experience affects the manner in which self concepts get implemented.

Purposes of Exploration

The fundamental purpose of vocational exploration is to enable the individual to grow in ability "to guide the unfolding of his career" (Super and Bohn, 1970). To do this he must understand and evaluate himself and his environment. More specific purposes, then, have to do with the accumulation of skills, attitudes, and awarenesses needed to define alternatives and make choices among them. The choosing person is the central figure in exploratory behavior.

Individual and Group Differences

It was seen above that differences exist among groups in various indices of vocational maturity. If a purpose of exploration is to maximize the individual's potential to choose, then group differences due to environmental causes have to be minimized. If opportunities for exploration are provided only in general terms, then those at advanced levels of maturity will progress rapidly while immature people progress slowly. The result will be the widening of differences. To avoid that outcome, exploratory experience needs to be planned specifically to address identified deficits.

Experiences may prove to be exploratory even when they are not planned to be. Professionals who intend to facilitate vocational development plan exploratory activities for students. In some cases, plans need to be tailored to individual learning styles or needs to provide maximum opportunity. Some students learn well through vicarious, abstract, or cognitive activity; others may require concrete hands-on involvement. It has been proposed (Cooley, 1964) that deficits in progress be identified early and corrected through specifically programmed experience. Individual differences in readiness to capitalize on exploration can be served by this means.

As can be expected from data about the relationship between

achievement and vocational maturity, working with nonachieving adolescents seeking employment often reveals deficiencies in basic academic skills. In one study of a remediation effort (Pope, 1966), reading instruction was found to be especially effective in the presence of personal interest on the part of a staff member. Most school personnel demonstrate personal interest in some students, but even casual observation suggests that it is not evenly distributed: some receive more than enough, and others, perhaps those who need it most, very little. If each staff member were to address some special attention to just a few students who need it, even if limited to a very specific purpose, the consequences could be very broad, especially if not everyone attends to the same students.

Exploration through Curriculum

All curriculum has the potential to serve exploratory purposes. Sometimes, that potential is not realized because of a failure to foster choosing (rather than requiring choices). Sometimes it is not realized simply because someone is not alert to the possibilities. Purposes of exploration will be more nearly assured if all individuals have opportunities for success.

Some rather extensive efforts to facilitate career development have been reviewed by Hansen (1970). One curriculum (New Jersey Department of Education, no date) is described as a vocational guidance program for all students, emphasizing short-term exploratory experience. In this program, field trips and contact with actual workers are common. The idea represented in this program is appealing and, intuitively, it is sound. Definitive evaluation is needed to determine its efficacy. Another program (Dreves, no date), Technology for Children, also has a great deal of appeal. The purpose is to provide elementary school children with psycho-motor and other experience related to the conditions and instruments of work. It is designed to be exploratory and facilitative of self-concept development. Outcomes, in this case, also need careful evaluation. Both of these programs have potential for serving exploratory purposes. Careful attention on the part of the teachers to bring explorational prospects into awareness at critical points would no doubt enhance productive exploration.

Counselors in consultation with teachers can suggest activities that will lend occupational relevance to typical classroom activities. As a result, some students may find more profitable opportunities for vocational exploration than would otherwise be available. It might be suggested that a literature class concerned with stereotypy focus on occupational rather than the usual personal stereotypes. A social issues lesson could take on occupational relevance by examining discrimination in terms of problems a city council may face in hiring a female business manager or promoting a nonwhite policeman to captain. An option for social studies reports might be a comparison of common occupational activities at various points in American history.

Imaginative counselors can help all teachers to find and use occupational points of focus in their subject matter. Some students respond with more interest if they know subject matter has occupational relevance. Teachers appreciate suggestions that spark student interest. A counselor and teacher planning together will probably see possibilities that neither would have identified on his own.

Exploration with Peers

In some cases, it has proved helpful to introduce opportunities for success through others close to the student's own age. Moon and Wilson (1970) used fifth graders to tutor first graders. Improvement was noted in self-confidence, trust, and a sense of competence. They also found that behavior improved and that there was growth in reading.

The possibilities to use age mates to provide success experiences in areas more specifically related to vocational behavior are many. Any sphere of behavior, not only the academic, can be the focus. One student who has mastered a skill can help another to learn it. Behaviors not ordinarily regarded as skills can be acquired the same way. One worker (or student) may help another to modify behavior in order to meet unaccustomed job expectations such as orderliness, punctuality, or teamwork.

Tseng (1972) proposed that employability can be increased by bridging the gap between perceived reality and objective reality. In the immediately preceding paragraphs, possibilities of using peers to initiate some bridge-building activities were considered. It may be possible to carry that process somewhat farther. Peers may be able to help one another to look at self-perceptions directly. Samler (1965) has suggested that self-awareness is a sound general educational objective. Peers may be more instrumental than adults, and especially authority figures, in promoting some kinds of self-awareness. Samler's suggestion of teaching behavior dynamics might also be used to provide a framework of knowledge within which students can work together in examining their developmental progress, academic and vocational alike. They can help one another learn that interpersonal behavior is predictable from self concepts (Thompson, 1972) but that specific self-perceptions are even better predictors (Fitts, 1972c). They can assist one another, perhaps, in developing motivation to change their own behavior and deciding on directions of change.

Guiding Exploration

The traditional activity of counselors has been individual counseling. Counseling with individuals can serve exploratory purposes well. Individuals can reconsider past events or plan future events in terms of opportunities to explore either themselves or their environments. Certain efforts to crystallize or clarify self-perceptions are probably most appropriately pursued in individual sessions.

Feedback about one's performance is a vital part of modifying one's self-perceptions. Because it sometimes needs to be handled delicately, it is best done individually. Reactions to evaluative judgments are not always as expected. Hills and Williams (1965) hypothesized that communication of educational-vocational test results would bring about positive changes in self-perceptions of clients in brief counseling. This expectation is consistent with what counselors often say about the value of this aspect of the work they do. It was found, however, that test results which differed from the client's preconceived notions had a negative effect. Furthermore, the reporting of test results, in general, did not lead to positive changes in self-perception. Fitts (1972c) found that all people respond more favorably to positive than to negative evaluation. He also found that response is more favorable to external evaluation when it is consistent with self-evaluation. As a matter of fact, subjects whose self-evaluation was positive responded favorably to any kind of feedback, but those whose self-evaluation was negative responded negatively to persons who gave additional negative evaluation. These findings indicate the importance of focusing on positive evaluations wherever possible.

Feedback to individuals does not come only in verbal form. Many things people do will offer opportunities for self-evaluation. It is in this connection that success experience is very important. Counseling can be used to help students plan experiences that maximize opportunities for success. Where success cannot be assured, the counselor may be helpful in anticipating possible failure and laying plans for how to face it and how to correct it. In a sense, the failure can be said to occur under supervision. Some experiences with high prospects of failure can be used specifically to serve as exploration, and if carefully planned, can work well.

Guiding the exploratory behavior of individuals is intended to facilitate their independent management of exploration. Use of group activities with students and consultation with teachers can serve to increase opportunities for self-direction. In all efforts to provide exploration, the purpose of helping individuals to develop into choosing persons is foremost. Whether by contemplation (Samler, 1965), by analysis of opportunities, trying out new experiences, or just doing nothing, the person makes choices. Exploration permits him to accumulate information about himself and his environment so that he can choose well.

Summary

This chapter considered several aspects of facilitating career development in schools. An important assumption was that researcher and practitioner can work together toward improving the quality of experience available to young people. In that connection, some hypotheses were suggested for possible investigation. Attention was directed to staff needs and information services. Vocational behavior, in terms of vocational maturity and self-perception, was discussed in more detail. The chapter closed with a discussion of exploration focusing on the central importance of fostering development of the mature choosing person as one who is ready for employment.

5

Toward the Improvement of Services

The Sixth Report of the National Advisory Council on Vocational Education (NACVE, 1972) cited above included several references ("sound" guidance practice, "effective" counseling, . . .) to the quality of performance in counseling and guidance programs. The statements in the Report sounded just as professional counselors often do, as if there were commonly accepted definitions of those qualities. The absence of such agreement may complicate what needs to be done to bring about improvement, but it does not justify failure to try.

Improvement of service to clients can be pursued by many routes, two of which will be treated in this final chapter: (1) conducting research designed to refine and expand knowledge; and (2) evaluating performance to determine whether purposes are achieved. Since the latter may lead to fundamental questions about guidance outcomes, a third section will consider a possible reconceptualization of what one of them should be.

Research and Employment of Youth

It is almost axiomatic to observe that school counselors do not attend sufficiently to research. Dugan (1960) concluded that it was a much neglected function. He charged both counselors and educators to extend the research done on all aspects of guidance. A decade later, Gamsky (1970) also found research neglected. Counselors usually give three major reasons for not doing more research in schools: (1) time; (2) lack of administrative support; and (3) inadequate research competency.

Research does consume time, it requires administrative approval, and it presumes some technical competence. In their requests to do research, counselors must attend to these concerns, but they must also not underestimate their own potential contribution. Because of its potential for helping to identify ways to spend time profitably, research should be among the high priorities for time allotments. Good design can help to gain support. Research needs to be done in schools even if it is not the classical experimental kind (Gamsky, 1970). Replication of other investigators' work may be a good beginning point for counselors. Replication is very much needed, and in some respects, it is easier to execute than original research.

Neglect of research in schools is not justified simply because it is difficult (Gamsky, 1970). Counselors need to be encouraged to find the time to do it, and to employ effective methods to gain administrative support. Technical assistance is sometimes more readily available than anticipated. Full use of all available resources to learn about factors which contribute to profitable employment of youth is an important method of improving service.

Evaluating the Outcomes of Vocational Guidance

In assessing the effectiveness of performance in vocational guidance, the most important criterion is what happens to the client as a result of the experience.

Long-Range Outcomes

Counselors want to be successful in the work they do. A fundamental purpose of vocational guidance programs is the facilitation of self-direction on the part of clients. It is assumed that if clients are helped to help themselves, then over the long run, their career behavior will be both more successful and more satisfying. If those outcomes occur, then counselors can consider themselves successful.

An important study of the long-range effects of counseling was done by Campbell (1965) who followed up, in 1962–63, 768 people who had been studied in the 1930s, by Williamson and Bordin. In the early study, counseled students made a better adjustment to college than noncounseled controls. Twenty-five years later (99 percent were located and 90 percent responded) the counseled group was found to be considerably more successful academically and slightly so in contribution to society. The National Institute of Industrial Psychology in England has also conducted studies demonstrating that young men who followed plans developed with counselors were more successful and better satisfied than others (Super and Bohn, 1970).

Short-Range Outcomes

As desirable as long-range outcomes are, the length of time that must pass before the evidence is in makes them unusable for some purposes. Short-range data are needed, too. When occupational success is used as a criterion, it is difficult to measure over the short run. Although placement in college or on a job has often been used as a criterion, it is obviously not a good measure of success. Many people who attain admission to college do not finish; first jobs are often unsuitable and tenure in them is short. Number of placements is also a poor criterion because it calls attention to disposition of cases rather than clients' direction of their own affairs. In effect, the focus is counselor input rather than client outcome.

Difficulty in demonstrating effectiveness in guidance, apparently, is one reason that counselors fall into the habit of trying to measure their own effort rather than what happens to clients. Statements reflecting that dilemma are often found among objectives for guidance programs: "To be available to students . . ." or "To counsel students . . ." or "To conduct career day. . . ." One advantage of such statements is that they are measurable. It is possible to report that a counselor was available for X number of hours, conducted Y counseling interviews, and supervised Z career day programs during a particular month. Compiling such information about a number of counselors' activities provides important quantified data. Counselors need to know how they spend their time.

A problem with the procedure just described is that the data become a source of temptation for demonstrating effectiveness. The distinction between how the counselor spends his time and the success or satisfaction of the client gets lost. The data about time use, i.e., counselor input, get used as if they were evidence of success.

One way to avoid the dilemma about short-range evidence of effectiveness is to seek different sources of data. Many schools conduct follow-up studies, and according to some observers (e.g., Kremer, 1970), with little profit. Usually, such studies offer graduates an opportunity to evaluate the service they received while still in school. That opportunity should be provided before they leave as well. Besides, a student who sees an opportunity to benefit directly from changes may be more motivated to contribute than one who sees the possible changes as benefiting only others. An additional dimension of candor can be gained by the suggested procedure that counselors interview students from one another's schools (Conn. ACES, 1966).

Anyone who has an interest in the outcomes of guidance programs is entitled to participate in determining program purposes. There is already confusion over what are suitable outcome criteria (Carey and Garris, 1971), so that specifying some in usable terms is likely to be difficult. Mueller (1959) identified the necessity to differentiate guidance purposes from educational purposes in general and to reduce their pretentiousness. Specifying guidance purposes that are unique would accomplish some reduction of pretentiousness. It is the appearance of trying to do everything that is unbelievable.

There is also confusion as to who should participate in which part of the process of determining outcomes and measuring whether they are accomplished. Decades of debate about roles and functions of counselors has done little to reduce the confusion. Some guidelines for examining outcomes are needed. It is assumed that counselors and others with whom they work can master the skills needed to write good outcome statements. The pressing need is for a conceptual framework within which to use them.

Conceptualizing Assessment of Outcomes

A primary reason that many years of debate about counselor role have not generated progress is because the wrong issue has been addressed (Kagan, 1964). Outcomes should be evaluated, not counselor behaviors. Conceptualizing a framework of outcome statements is the first step in the process of evaluation.

It is useful to conceptualize three different kinds of outcome statements. They are different in part because the criteria by which they can be measured require different lengths of time to mature. But there is another difference, a qualitative one, a matter of scope rather than time. These differences are important because they affect the means of measurement. To facilitate the discussion of differences the terms *purpose, goal,* and *objective* will be used. They are not entirely satisfactory terms, but they will serve well enough.

In the simplest terms, an objective is seen as measurable by direct observation of behavior, a goal as measurable through inferences from observable behavior, and a purpose as measurable only by analysis of the relationships among many behaviors. A parallel can be seen between these and short-, intermediate-, and long-range outcomes, but the essential difference is the complexity of the criterion, not the time.

A concrete example can be found in relation to occupational information as an index of vocational maturity. A possible *objective* is collection of information. Criteria would be student behaviors related to information collection—using a trade school bulletin, interviewing a worker, taking notes while on a field trip, requesting test scores, etc. A related *goal* is the application of the information in some decision-making activity—applying for a particular job, dropping a course, changing an expressed occupational preference. The *purpose* is to achieve a satisfactory ultimate vocational adjustment, which is obviously distant and difficult to measure.

Another difference among the outcome statements is the manner in which they are determined. As indicated above, anybody who has an interest may participate in determining purposes. In practice, in a school setting, administrators will usually be active in helping to determine goals; they may or may not be active in formulating objectives. In any case, once outcomes are agreed upon, it is the responsibility of the counselor to determine which behaviors he will employ to accomplish the outcomes (goals and objectives) with which he is charged. The administrator and counselor agree upon criteria for each, and relative attainment of the criteria is the basis for assessing performance. In some cases, immediate feedback may help a counselor to modify his behaviors on rather short notice.

The different outcome statements also vary in the readiness with which they submit to behavioral descriptions. Objectives are relatively simple to translate into behavioral terms and are, therefore, readily measured. Goals may be describable behaviorally or they may not. Goals which are concerned with appreciations, awarenesses, or other more clearly affective responses may be particularly difficult to state behaviorally. It is important to note that behavioral statements of outcome are not always necessary. Important outcomes should not be overlooked because evaluators have not learned to express them in behavioral terms (Katz, 1971). Purposes are especially difficult to translate into measurable descriptions of behavior.

As agreement is reached on suitable outcomes of guidance programs, it will be possible to determine, with greater assurance than has been the case in the past, which competencies counselors need. Then preparation can be geared to the job.

The Choosing Person

In the formulations presented here, the choosing person has been a central concept. It is postulated that self-actualization through career behavior becomes possible as an individual evaluates himself and his environment, identifies alternative courses of action for implementation of self-attributes, and chooses among them. All choosing behavior occurs within the broad limits established by physical and environmental factors.

Potential to become self-actualizing through occupational implementation is not equally distributed among people because those environmental forces impinge differently on some than they do on others. The potential to choose is different for some than for others, not only with regard to the number of choices but the quality of choices as well. Many have observed that counselors pay insufficient heed to environmental determinants of behavior. Gordon (1971) has proposed attention to them in ways that suggest significant changes in the operation of guidance programs. He proposed several shifts in guidance activities to expand alternatives for choice and to optimize decision behavior for all.

Although Gordon's concern was general development, his suggestions have important implications for career development as well. The vocational counselor who would optimize opportunities for satisfying employment for all youth must give serious consideration (1) to methods of helping young people to cope with the environmental forces that shape their career opportunities; and (2) to working with youth in devising ways to create circumstances that permit vocational maturation to occur for all. These efforts will insure that increasing numbers of individuals are prepared to guide the unfolding of their own careers.

Summary

This chapter considered briefly the importance of research and evaluation as means of improving the quality of vocational guidance services. A conceptual framework was offered for consideration of the outcomes of guidance and a reconceptualization of some ways to accomplish one of the central outcomes was suggested.

BIBLIOGRAPHY

Adams, J. F. Adolescent personal problems as a function of age and sex. *Journal of Genetic Psychology*, 1964, 104, 207–214.

American Personnel and Guidance Association. *Program summaries and abstracts: 1971 convention.* Washington, D.C.: APGA, 1971a.

_____. *Research reports: 1971 convention.* Washington, D.C.: APGA, 1971b.

_____. *1972 APGA Convention Program.* Washington, D.C.: APGA, 1972a.

_____. *APGA membership report.* Washington, D.C.: APGA, 1972b, Mimeo.

American School Counselors Association. *Policy for secondary school counselors,* Washington, D.C.: APGA, 1964.

Anandam, K. and Williams, R. L. A model for consultation with classroom teachers on behavior management. *The School Counselor,* 1971, 18, 253–259.

Anderson, J. E. Dynamics of development: system in process, in O. B. Harris (Ed.), *The concept of development.* Minneapolis: University of Minnesota Press, 1957.

Ansell, E. M. and Hansen, J. C. Patterns in vocational development of urban youth. *Journal of Counseling Psychology,* 1971, 18, 505–508.

Arbuckle, D. S. Does the school really need counselors? *The School Counselor,* 1970, 17, 325–330.

Astin, H. S. Career development of girls during the high school years. *Journal of Counseling Psychology,* 1968, 15, 536–540.

Atkinson, J. W. *An introduction to motivation.* Princeton, N.J.: Van Nostrand, 1964.

Bailey, S. T. Independence and factor structure of self-concept metadimensions. *Journal of Counseling Psychology,* 1970, 17, 425–430.

Bingham, W. C. Change of occupation as a function of the regnancy of occupational self concepts. Unpublished doctoral dissertation, Teachers College, Columbia University, 1966.

_____. *Counseling services for unemployed youth.* New York: Center for the Study of Unemployed Youth, 1967.

_____. Career model: singular or plural? *Counseling Psychologist,* 1969a, 1, 32–34.

_____. Job satisfaction in employment counselors. *Journal of Employment Counseling,* 1969b, 6, 79–83.

Blocher, D. H. and Shutz, R. A. Relationships among self-descriptions, occupational sterotypes, and vocational preferences. *Journal of Counseling Psychology,* 1961, 8, 314–317.

77

Bohn, M. J., Jr. Counselor behavior as a function of counselor dominance, counselor experience and client type. *Journal of Counseling Psychology*, 1965, 12, 346–352.

Borow, H. (Ed.). *Man in a world at work*. Boston: Houghton Mifflin, 1964.

Brenner, M. H. Use of high school data to predict work performance. *Journal of Applied Psychology*, 1968, 52, 29–30.

Brewer, J. M. *The vocational-guidance movement: its problems and possibilities*. New York: Macmillan, 1918.

————. *Education as guidance*. New York: The Macmillan Company, 1932.

————, *et al. Case studies in educational and vocational guidance*. New York: Ginn, 1926.

————, *et al. History of vocational guidance*. New York: Harper, 1942.

Brough, J. R. A profile of junior high school counseling. *The School Counselor*, 1969, 17, 67–72.

Brown, L. M. Justifying our existence. *The School Counselor*, 1971, 19, 9–10.

Burnett, C. W. Selections and training of school and college personnel workers. *Review of Educational Research*, 1954, 24, 121–133.

Campbell, D. P. Achievements of counseled and non-counseled students twenty-five years after counseling. *Journal of Counseling Psychology*, 1965, 12, 287–293.

Carey, A. R. and Garris, D. L. Accountability for school counselors. *The School Counselor*, 1971, 18, 321–326.

Carkhuff, R., Alexik, Mae, and Anderson, Susan. Do we have a theory of vocational choice? *Personnel and Guidance Journal*, 1967, 46, 335–345.

Carmical, LaVerne and Calvin, L. Jr. Functions selected by school counselors. *The School Counselor*, 1970, 17, 280–285.

Casky, O. L. Teacher inconsistency and guidance readiness. *Journal of Counseling Psychology*, 1960, 7, 58–61.

Conant, J. B. *The American high school today*. New York: McGraw-Hill, 1959.

Connecticut Association for Counselor Education and Supervision, *et al.* An investigation of factors related to the image of the school counselor in Connecticut. College of Education, University of Bridgeport, 1966, (Mimeo).

Cooley, W. W. A Computer-measurement system for guidance. *Harvard Educational Review*, 1964, 34, 559–572.

Coopersmith, S. A method for determining types of self-esteem. *Journal of Abnormal and Social Psychology*, 1959, 59, 87–94.

Crites, J. O. *The maturity of vocational attitudes in adolescence*. Iowa City: University of Iowa, 1969 (a).

————. *Vocational psychology*. New York: McGraw-Hill, 1969 (b).

Davies, Nancy. Vocational guidance — an educational Topsy. *The School Guidance Worker*, 1971, 27, No. 2, 12–20.

Davis, D. A. Counseling and vocational education. *The Vocational Guidance Quarterly*, 1960, 9, 37–40.

Dreves, Fred J. *Technology for children project: rationale.* Trenton: New Jersey State Department of Education, undated.

Drews, Elizabeth. Counseling for self-actualization in gifted girls and young women. *Journal of Counseling Psychology,* 1965, 12, 167–185.

Dugan, W. E. The organization and administration of guidance services. *Review of Educational Research,* 1960, 30, 105–114.

Ekman, P., Friessen, W. V., and Lutzker, D. R. Psychological reactions to infantry basic training. *Journal of Consulting Psychology,* 1962, 26, 103–104.

Englander, Meryl. A psychological analysis of vocational choice: teaching. *Journal of Counseling Psychology,* 1960, 7, 257–264.

Engle, K. B. and Betz, R. L. A two-year program of counselor education. *Counselor Education and Supervision,* 1971, 10, 171–179.

Evans, J. R., and Cody, J. J. Transfer of decision-making skills learned in a counseling-like setting to similar and dissimilar situations. *Journal of Counseling Psychology,* 1969, 16, 427–432.

Falik, L. H., Grimm, M., Preston, F., and Konno, T. Evaluating the impact of the counseling-learning team on the elementary school. *The School Counselor,* 1971, 18, 25–37.

Fitts, W. H. *The self concept and psychopathology.* Nashville, Tenn.: Dede Wallace Center (Monograph IV), 1972a.

_____. *The self concept and performance.* Nashville, Tenn.: Dede Wallace Center (Monograph V), 1972b.

_____. *The self concept and behavior: overview and supplement.* Nashville, Tenn.: Dede Wallace Center (Monograph VII), 1972c.

Ford, Susan F. An investigation of values for and processing of vocational information by high school students and counselors: a mathematical approach. Unpublished doctoral dissertation, Rutgers University, 1969.

Freeberg, N. E. *Development of evaluation measures for use with Neighborhood Youth Corps enrollees.* Princeton, N.J.: Educational Testing Service, 1968.

Fretz, B. B. Predicting career preference from preadolescent development. *Journal of Counseling Psychology,* 1972, 19, 286–291.

Gamsky, N. R. Action research and the school counselor. *The School Counselor,* 1970, 18, 36–42.

Gannon, F. B. Counselors in action. *The School Counselor,* 1965, 13, 39–41.

Gillham, Isabel. Self-concept and reading. *The Reading Teacher,* 1967, 21, 270–273.

Ginzberg, E., Ginsburg, S., Axelrad, S., and Herma, J. L. *Occupational choice.* New York: Columbia University Press, 1951.

Ginzberg, E. Guidance: an interdisciplinary approach. Paper read at the 24th Rutgers Guidance Conference, October, 1967.

Gold, Sandra O. The effect of counselor-client dissimilarity on counselor judgment. Unpublished doctoral dissertation, Rutgers University, 1970.

Gordon, E. W. Perspectives on counseling and other approaches to guided behavior change. *The Counseling Psychologist,* 1971, 3, 1–9.

Gowan, J. C. Organization of guidance for the gifted. *Personnel and Guidance Journal*, 1960, 39, 275–279.

Gribbons, W. D. Evaluation of an eighth grade group guidance program. *Personnel and Guidance Journal*, 1960, 38, 740–745.

————, and Lohnes, P. R. Predicting five years of development in adolescents from readiness for vocational planning scales. *Journal of Educational Psychology*, 1965, 56, 244–253.

————. *Emerging careers: a study of 111 adolescents*. New York: Teachers College Press, 1968.

Grundfest, Sandra. The effect of student teaching and related professional training on vocational self-concept development. In American Personnel and Guidance Association, *Research Reports: 1971 Convention*. Washington, D. C.: APGA, 1971, pp. 73–74.

Haettenschwiller, D. L. Control of the counselor's role. *Journal of Counseling Psychology*, 1970, 17, 437–442.

————, and Jabs, W. The counselor and the instructional program. *The School Counselor*, 1969, 17, 118–125.

Hansen, Lorraine S. *Career guidance practices in school and community*. Washington, D.C.: National Vocational Guidance Association, 1970.

Havener, P. H. and Izard, C. E. Unrealistic self-enhancement in paranoid schizophrenics. *Journal of Consulting Psychology*, 1962, 26, 65–68.

Havighurst, Robert J. *Human development and education*. New York: Longmans, Green, 1953.

Herzberg, F., Mausner, B., and Snyderman, B. *The motivation to work*. New York: Wiley, 1959.

Hewer, Vivian H. Vocational interests of college freshmen and their social origins. *Journal of Applied Psychology*, 1965, 49, 407–411.

Hill, G. E., and Nitzschke, D. F. Preparation programs in elementary school guidance. *Personnel and Guidance Journal*, 1961, 40, 155–159.

Hills, D. A. and Williams, J. E. Effects of test information upon self-evaluation in brief educational-vocational counseling. *Journal of Counseling Psychology*, 1965, 12, 275–281.

Hirning, L. C. B. Sound trends and appropriate ambitions of the counseling movement. *Teachers College Record*, 1944, 46, 25–33.

Hollender, J. W. Development of vocational decisions during adolescence. *Journal of Counseling Psychology*, 1971, 18, 244–248.

Hume, Laurabel N. Is there a typical employment counselor? *Journal of Employment Counseling*, 1967, 4, 127–131.

Humes, C. W. Jr. Are counselors part of pupil personnel services? *The School Counselor*, 1971, 18, 316–391.

Indik, B. P. Measuring motivation to work. *Personnel Administration*, 1966, 40, 39–44 (a).

————. *The motivation to work*. New Brunswick, N.J.: Institute of Management and Labor Relations, Rutgers University, 1966 (b).

————, and Seymore, J. *Results of the occupational exposure program.*

Institute of Management and Labor Relations, Rutgers University, New Brunswick, N.J., 1969, (mimeo).

Jones, A. J. and Miller, L. M. The national picture of pupil personnel and guidance services in 1953. *National Association of Secondary School Principals Bulletin*, 1954, 38, 105–159.

Jordaan, Jean P. Exploratory behavior: the formation of self and occupational concepts, in Super, D. E., *et al.* (Eds.), *Career development: self concept theory.* New York: College Entrance Examination Board, 1963.

———. The prediction of early adult vocational behavior. New York: Teachers College, Columbia University, 1972 (Mimeo).

Joseph, E. A. and Drury, W. R. Ohio counselors evaluate their formal preparation. *Counselor Education and Supervision*, 1971, 11, 56–61.

Kagan, N. Three dimensions of counselor encapsulation. *Journal of Counseling Psychology*, 1964, 11, 361–365.

Kaplan, H. H. A case for better training in pre-college guidance: Counselors speak out. *Pre-service and in-service preparation of school counselors for educational guidance.* Washington, D.C.: American Personnel and Guidance Association, 1970.

Katz, M. R. Evaluating guidance — why, what, and how, in Bingham, William C. (Ed.), *Accountability: process and product.* Proceedings of the 28th Rutgers Guidance Conference, Rutgers University, New Brunswick, N.J., 1971.

Kelly, G. A. *The psychology of personal constructs* Vol. 1. New York: Norton, 1955.

Ketterman, C. S. The opinion of selected publics concerning the school counselor's function. *The School Counselor*, 1969, 16, 41–45, 49.

Kitson, H. D. Getting rid of a piece of educational rubbish. *Teachers College Record*, 1934, 36, 30–34.

Koos, L. V. and Kefauver, G. N. *Guidance in secondary schools.* New York: Macmillan, 1932.

Korman, A. K. The self-esteem variable in vocational choice. *Journal of Applied Psychology*, 1966, 50, 479–486.

———. Self-esteem as a moderator of the relationship between self-perceived abilities and vocational choice. *Journal of Applied Psychology*, 1967, 51, 65–67 (a).

———. The relevance of personal need satisfaction for overall satisfaction as a function of self-esteem. *Journal of Applied Psychology*, 1967, 51, 533–538 (b).

———. Self-esteem as a moderator in vocational choice. *Journal of Applied Psychology*, 1969, 53, 188–192.

Kratochvil, D. W., Jones, G. B. and Ganschow, Laurie H. Helping students to help themselves. *The School Counselor*, 1970, 17, 376–383.

Kremer, B. J. Follow-up? — Forget it! *The School Counselor*, 1970, 17, 228–232.

Kuder, G. F. *Profile sheet, Kuder Preference Record, Vocational, Form C.* Chicago: Science Research Associates, 1951.

————. *Examiner manual, Kuder Preference Record, Vocational, Form C.* Chicago: Science Research Associates, 1956.

Kushel, G. The counselor's image and the chameleon. *The School Counselor,* 1970, 17, 286–291.

LeMay, M. L. and Damm, V. J. The personal orientation inventory as a measure of the self-actualization of under-achievers. *Measurement and Evaluation in Guidance,* 1968, 1, 110–114.

Leonard, G. E., Jefferies, Doris, and Spedding, Sally. *Doctor, lawyer, Indian chief: a career guidance manual for elementary teachers.* Detroit: Development Career Guidance Project, 1968.

Lewellyn, L. W., and Grace, H. A. Real vocational help from academic advisors. *Vocational Guidance Quarterly,* 1969, 9, 25–27.

Lewis, E. C. Counselors and girls. *Journal of Counseling Psychology,* 1965, 12, 159–166.

Lewis, M. D. and Lewis, Judith A. Relevant training for relevant roles: A model for educating inner city counselors. *Counselor Education and Supervision,* 1970, 10, 31–38.

LoCascio, R. Delayed and impaired vocational development: A neglected aspect of vocational development theory. *Personnel and Guidance Journal,* 1964, 42, 885–887.

Lundquist, G. W., and Chamley, J. C. Counselor-consultant: A move toward effectiveness. *The School Counselor,* 1971, 18, 362–366.

MacArthur, R. S. and Mosychuk, H. Lower and upper socioeconomic group contrasts in long-term predictability of grade nine achievement. *Journal of Educational Measurement,* 1966, 3, 167–168.

MacMinn, P. and Ross, R. G. *Status of preparation programs for guidance and personnel workers.* Washington, D.C.: U. S. Department of Health, Education, and Welfare, Office of Education, 1959.

Maslow, A. *Motivation and personality.* New York: Harper, 1954.

Matthewson, R. H. *Guidance policy and practice.* New York: Harper, 1st ed., 1949.

Mayer, G. R. and Carlson, J. Fading: A behavioral procedure to increase independent behavior. *The School Counselor,* 1971, 18, 193–197.

Maynard, P. E., and Hansen, J. C. Vocational maturity among inner-city youth. *Journal of Counseling Psychology,* 1970, 17, 400–404.

McCall, J. N. Masculine striving as a clue to skilled-trade interests. *Journal of Applied Psychology,* 1965, 49, 106–109.

McGee, S. E. Fifth-grade boys' self-esteem as a function of teacher expectations. Unpublished doctoral dissertation, Rutgers University, 1971.

McNeil, E. B. Is counseling a rat fink operation? *Psychology in the schools,* 1965, 2, 24–31.

Miller, Carroll H. Vocational guidance in the perspective of cultural change, in Borow, H. (ed.), *Man in a world of work.* Boston. Houghton Mifflin, 1964.

Miller, D. C. and Form, W. H. *Industrial Sociology.* New York: Harper, 1951.

Miner, W. R. An evaluation of criticism concerned with the self report. New York: Career Pattern Study, Teachers College, Columbia University, 1963, (Mimeo).

Moon, Mozetta and Wilson, Doris. Teacher–counselor cooperation: building self-concepts and confidence in children. *The School Counselor,* 1970, 17, 364–366.

Mueller, Kate H. Criteria for evaluating professional status. *Personnel and Guidance Journal,* 1959, 37, 410–417.

Myers, G. E. Relationship between vocational and educational guidance. *News Bulletin of the American Vocational Association,* 1933, 8, 15–17.

Myers, R. A. The content and character of training programs in counseling psychology, in Thompson, A. S. and Super, D. E. (Eds.), *The professional preparation of counseling psychologists.* New York: Bureau of Publications, Teachers College, Columbia Univ., 1964.

National Advisory Council on Vocational Education. Counseling and guidance: A call for change. Washington, D.C.: NACVE, 1972, (Mimeo).

Neale, D. C. and Proshek, J. M. School-related attitudes of culturally disadvantaged elementary school children. *Journal of Educational Psychology,* 1967, 58, 238–244.

Neel, Elsie O. Preparing students for employment. *The School Counselor,* 1971, 18, 294–296.

New Jersey State Department of Education. *Introduction to vocation: guidelines and policies.* Trenton: author, undated.

Newman, H. Follow-up study of thirty-four vocational high school dropouts. *The School Counselor,* 1966, 13, 207–212.

Norris, Willa. More than a decade of training guidance and personnel workers. *Personnel and Guidance Journal,* 1960, 39, 287–291.

Novick, B. Teachers guide to the effective use of community speakers. Woodbridge, N.J.: Central Jersey Industry-Education Council, 1968, (Mimeo).

————. Field trips: A teacher's guide. Woodbridge, N.J.: Central Jersey Industry-Education Council, 1969, (Mimeo).

O'Hara, R. P. Comment on Super's papers. *The Counseling Psychologist,* 1969, 1, 29–31.

Oppenheimer, E. A. A self-concept approach to predicting occupational preferences. Unpublished doctoral dissertation, Teachers College, Columbia, University, 1964.

Osgood, C. E., Suci, G. J., and Tannenbaum, P. H. *The measurement of meaning.* Urbana: The University of Illinois Press, 1957.

Parsons, F. *Choosing a vocation.* Boston: Houghton Mifflin Company, 1909.

Paterson, D. C. and Lofquist, L. H. A note on the training of clinical and counseling psychologists. *American Psychologist,* 1960, 15, 365–366.

Patterson, C. H. Subprofessional functions and short-term training. *Counselor Education and Supervision,* 1965, 4, 144–146.

Pope, Lillie. A reading program for school dropouts. *Journal of Reading*, 1966, 9, 367–378.

Rampel, Marion. A metadimensional approach to occupational choice: regnancy and the translation model. Unpublished doctoral dissertation, Rutgers University, 1967.

Roe, Anne, Hubbard, W. D., Hutchinson, T., and Bateman, T. Studies of occupational histories: Part I. Job changes and the classification of occupations. *Journal of Counseling Psychology*, 1966, 13, 387–393.

Roeber, E. C. *Orientation to the job of a counselor*. Chicago: Science Research Associates, 1961.

Rose, Harriett A., and Elton, C. F. Sex and occupational choice. *Journal of Counseling Psychology*, 1971, 18, 456–461.

Rossi, Alice. Women in science: why so few? *Science*, 1965, 148, 1196–1202.

Rousseve, R. J. Toward an epitaph for the 'nonjudgmental' educator-counselor. *The School Counselor*, 1971, 19, 4–8.

Russell, J. W. Vocational guidance preparation needs an overhaul. *The Vocational Guidance Quarterly*, 1960, 9, 45–47.

Samler, J. The school and self-understanding. *Harvard Educational Review*, 1965, 35, 55–70.

Schlossberg, Nancy K. Sub-professionals: to be or not to be. *Counselor Education and Supervision*, 1967, 6, 108–113.

Seim, R. M. Night counseling. *The School Counselor*, 1970, 17, 172–174.

Shappell, D. L., Hall, L. G., and Tarrier, R. B. Perceptions of the world of work. *Journal of Counseling Psychology*, 1971, 18, 55–59.

Shiner, E. V. Self concepts of individuals in the process of changing occupations. Unpublished doctoral dissertation, Teachers College, Columbia University, 1963.

Shultz, J. L. A cross-sectional study of development, dimensionality, and correlates of the self concept in school age boys. Unpublished doctoral dissertation, University of Iowa, 1965.

Siegel, Betty. Counseling the color-conscious. *The School Counselor*, 1970, 17, 168–170.

Siggers, Kathleen. Relationships between occupational self concept, occupational role concept, and occupational role performance. Unpublished doctoral dissertation, Rutgers University, 1971.

Snygg, D. and Combs, A. W. *Individual behavior*. New York: Harper, 1949.

Spears, M. J., Jensen, G. W., and Kindres, L. W. How can we make the best use of the time and energies of the guidance counselors we now have? *National Association of Secondary School Principals Bulletin*, 1961, 45, 302–307.

Starishevsky, R. and Matlin, N. A model for the translation of self concepts into vocational terms, in Super, Donald E., *et al.* (Eds.), *Career development: self concept theory*. New York: College Entrance Examination Board, 1963.

Stephenson, R. R. Occupational choice as a crystallized self concept. *Journal of Counseling Psychology*, 1961, 8, 211–216.

Stoughton, R. W. The preparation of counselors and personnel workers. *Review of Educational Research*, 1957, 27, 174–185.

Strowig, R. W. News from the university of Wisconsin. *Guidelines*, Wisconsin State Department of Public Instruction, Madison, 1963, 1, 20–21.

Super, D. E. Vocational adjustment: implementing a self-concept. *Occupations*, 1951, 30, 88–92.

————. A theory of vocational development. *American Psychologist*, 1953, 8, 185–190.

————. *Psychology of careers.* New York: Harper, 1957.

————. Self concepts in vocational development, in Super, D. E. *et al.* (Eds.), *Career development: self concept theory.* New York: College Entrance Examination Board, 1963a.

————. Toward making self-concept theory operational. In Super, D. E. *et al.* (Eds.), *Career development: self concept theory.* New York: College Entrance Examination Board, 1963b.

————. Vocational development theory: persons, positions, and processes. *The Counseling Psychologist*, 1969, 1, 2–14.

————. Vocational maturity theory and the career development inventory: implementing a psychology of careers in career guidance. New York: Teachers College, Columbia University, 1972, (Mimeo).

————, and Bohn, M. J., Jr. *Occupational psychology.* Belmont, Calif.: Wadsworth, 1970.

————, and others. *Vocational development: A framework for research.* New York: Bureau of Publications, Teachers College, Columbia University, 1957.

————, and Forrest, D. J. *Career development inventory, Form 1, preliminary manual.* New York: Teachers College, Columbia University, 1972.

————, and Jordaan, J. P. *Career development theory.* New York: Teachers College, Columbia University, 1972 (Mimeo).

————, and Overstreet, P. *The vocational maturity of ninth-grade boys.* New York: Bureau of Publications, Teachers College, Columbia University, 1960.

————, Starishevsky, R., Matlin, N., and Jordaan, J. P. *Career development: self concept theory.* New York: College Entrance Examination Board, 1963.

Thompson, A. S. and Super, D. E. (Eds.). *The professional preparation of counseling psychologists.* New York: Bureau of Publications, Teachers College, Columbia University, 1964.

Thompson, W. *Correlates of the self concept.* Nashville, Tenn.: Dede Wallace Center (Monograph VI), 1972.

Tiedeman, D. V. and O'Hara, R. P. *Career development: choice and adjustment.* New York: College Entrance Examination Board, 1963.

Trotzer, J. P. and Kassera, W. J. Do counselors do what they are taught? *The School Counselor*, 1971, 18, 335–341.

Tseng, M. S. Self-perception and employability: A vocational rehabilitation problem. *Journal of Counseling Psychology*, 1972, 19, 314–317.

Tyler, L. E. *The work of the counselor*, 2nd ed. New York: Appleton-Century-Crofts, Inc., 1961.

Vacchiano, R. B., Strauss, P. S., and Schiffman, D. C. Personality correlates of dogmatism. *Journal of Consulting and Clinical Psychology*, 1968, 32, 83–85.

Vassos, Sonya T. The utilization of peer influence. *The School Counselor*, 1971, 18, 209–214.

Vriend, J. Vocational maturity ratings of inner-city high school seniors. *Journal of Counseling Psychology*, 1969, 16, 377–384.

Warren, J. R. Self concept, occupational role expectation, and change of college major. *Journal of Counseling Psychology*, 1961, 8, 164–169.

Weil, P. E. The holding power of a work-study high school for dropouts. Unpublished doctoral dissertation, Rutgers University, 1970.

Wertheim, Judith B. The vocational development of non-college-bound high school students: application of a self-concept theory. Unpublished doctoral dissertation, Rutgers University, 1971.

Witczak, Lois A. and Ehlers, Dorothy. Project: occupational orientation. *The School Counselor*, 1970, 17, 362–363.

Wrenn, C. G. Trends and predictions in vocational guidance. *Occupations*, 1947, 25, 503–515.

————. Status and role of the school counselor. *Personnel and Guidance Journal*, 1957, 36, 175–183.

Wylie, Ruth. *The self concept*. Lincoln, Nebr.: University Nebraska Press, 1961.

INDEX

....

DATE DUE

APR 24 1978		
NOV 1 1982		
NOV 15 1982		
FEB 21 1983		
APR 15 1985		
GAYLORD		PRINTED IN U.S.A.